WALKING IN THE DRAKENSBERG

About the author

After a short-service commission in the Army, Jeff Williams trained in Paediatric medicine and subsequently worked as a consultant paediatrician at a hospital in North Wales for 30 years. During that time he researched and wrote walking and climbing guides to the Stubai Alps, Silvretta Alps and Ötztaler Alps in Europe.

After retirement he trained and qualified as a Safari Guide in South Africa. Currently he lectures on guiding and bird-watching, dividing his time between North Wales and, because of his love affair with the country and its people, South Africa.

Other Cicerone guides by the author
Walking in the Ardennes

WALKING IN THE DRAKENSBERG

75 DAY WALKS

by Jeff Williams

2 POLICE SQUARE, MILNTHORPE, CUMBRIA LA7 7PY
www.cicerone.co.uk

© Jeff Williams 2017
Second edition 2017
ISBN 978 1 85284 881 5

First edition 2010

Printed by KHL Printing, Singapore.

A catalogue record for this book is available from the British Library.

All photographs are by Maryann and Jeff Williams with the exception of the following: pp29 (middle), 97, 120, 141, 147, 155, 165 – Patricia Goodwin; p21 (lower) – Stuart McLean; p98 – Jason Stanley and p114 – Angus MacLaren (www.traverseline.co.uk).

Dedication

This book is for my grandchildren Joshua, Sam, Carys, Thomas, Oliver, Rosie and George. I hope that mountains, the outdoors and nature generally give them as much pleasure as it has given me and that they will, sometime in the future, get to experience the wonders of Southern Africa and the warmth of its people.

Updates to this guide

While every effort is made by our authors to ensure the accuracy of guide-books as they go to print, changes can occur during the lifetime of an edition. Any updates that we know of for this guide will be on the Cicerone website (www.cicerone.co.uk/881/updates), so please check before planning your trip. We also advise that you check information about such things as transport, accommodation and shops locally. Even rights of way can be altered over time. We are always grateful for information about any discrepancies between a guidebook and the facts on the ground, sent by email to info@cicerone.co.uk or by post to Cicerone, 2 Police Square, Milnthorpe LA7 7PY, United Kingdom.

Front cover: The Amphitheatre in the Royal Natal National Park seen from Thendele camp (Walks 7 and 8)

CONTENTS

WARNING

Mountaineering and wilderness trekking can be dangerous activities carrying a risk of personal injury or death. It should be undertaken only by those with a full understanding of the risks and with the training and/or experience to evaluate them. Mountaineers and trekkers should be appropriately equipped for the routes undertaken. Every care and effort has been taken in the preparation of this book, but the user should be aware that conditions can be highly variable and can change quickly, thus materially affecting the seriousness of a climb, tour or expedition.

Therefore, except for any liability which cannot be excluded by law, neither Cicerone nor the authors accept liability for damage of any nature (including damage to property, personal injury or death) arising directly or indirectly from the information in this book.

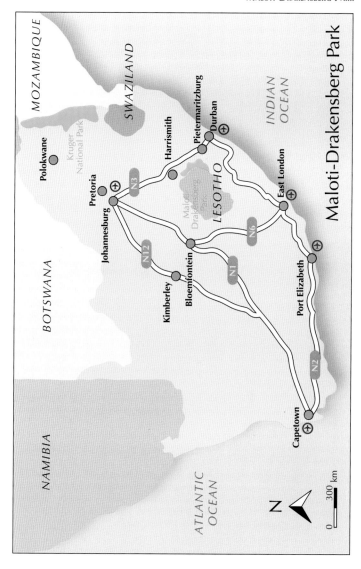

Acknowledgements

It is customary to say that thanking each person by name who contributed to a publication is infeasible because of constraints of space. Sadly, this is true here too. I trust that those whose names are not included will forgive the omission.

Books only get into print because of publishers. Jonathan Williams has assembled a helpful and friendly team at Cicerone and I am pleased to acknowledge their huge expertise. Particular thanks are due to my editor Clare Shaw who, in her painstaking review of the maps and manuscript, was a model of tact when suggesting sensible and necessary adjustments.

A big thank you is due to all those people who I encountered on the survey trips at bush camps, in hotels, even airports, but especially on the trail for their friendship, comments and encouragement.

Errol Cunnama, the then Entertainments Manager at Cathedral Peak Hotel, gave me great assistance in organisational terms as did Megan Bedingham at The Cavern Drakensberg Resort and Spa. Also, Stephen Richert, conservation manager in The Royal Natal National Park, gave generously of his time to talk through a number of issues with me.

I was fortunate in having a great bunch of companions on some of the walks. The guides Moses (Cathedral Peak Hotel) and Cedric and Wonder Boy (at Monk's Cowl) provided great support on challenging journeys in the high mountains. The days I spent exploring the Cobham area with guides Stuart McLean, Paul Roth and the late Ian Foster, all of Himeville, were amusing as well as instructive and the folk of the Sani Hiking Club delightful to walk with as well as being veritable mines of information on all things Drakensberg-related. Stuart and his wife Helga were very helpful in suggesting amendments to the manuscript where I had erred in nomenclature or spelling. Ron Tavener-Smith (lately Professor of Geology in Durban) was my adviser on the geology section and gave permission for the use of his original diagram.

My good friend Patricia Goodwin gave up four weeks of her time to accompany me on two survey visits which were tough but exhilarating and enormous fun. A number of the photographs are hers.

Finally, but most importantly, I come to my wife Maryann. She, with the forbearance that you need after many years of marriage to an obsessional eccentric, spent six arduous weeks on the trail including a 4-week incident-rich stint during which we covered 300km with over 13000m height gain and only two days' respite but still finished enthusiastic and smiling. Apart from tolerating my absences from home and 'book focus time' she took nearly all the photographs and did the time-consuming and painstaking job of preparing them for publication. Great job!

Map Key

═══ N3 ═══	major road		marsh
═══════	minor road	♠	hotel
– – – – –	route	■	building
··············	alt route or major footpath	≍	pass
··············	unmetalled road	∗	viewpoint
─ ─ ─ ─	national boundary	↙	direction arrow
∼∼∼∼	ridge	↙	route direction arrow
∼∼∼	river	Å	camp
∼∼∼	seasonal river	©	cave
●	town/village	W	waterfall
○	place of interest	◠	lake
·	spot height	○	park entrance
▲	peak		
⊸⊸⊸	cliff		
❶	route number		
P	parking		
⊸⊸⊸	steep ground		
⊓	ladder		
🌲	forest		

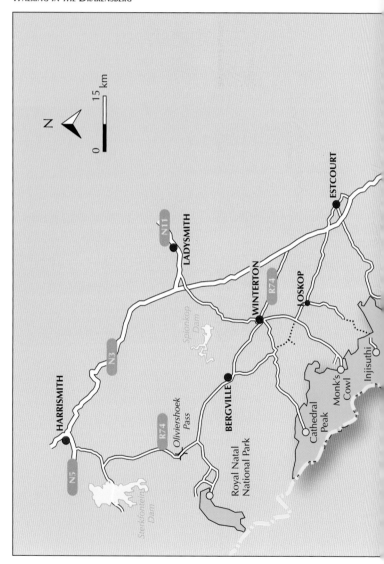

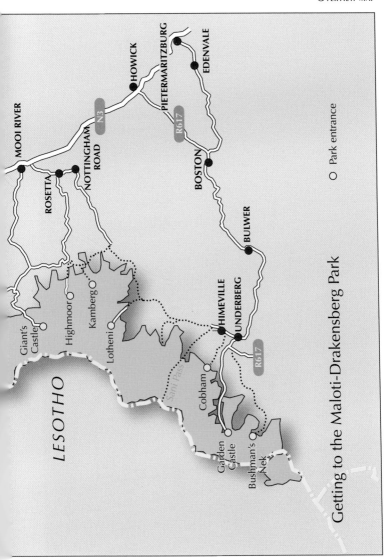

Getting to the Maloti-Drakensberg Park

○ Park entrance

On the Contour Path below the Outer and Inner Horns (Walk 24)

INTRODUCTION

'The Boer and his son gazed up at the massive, seemingly vertical, rock wall of the peak above them, the top shrouded in cloud as all the peaks were that day. High above they saw clearly a giant lizard with a long tail and wings flying easily across the sky. They called the mountains in their Afrikaaner language the *Drakensberg* – the Dragon's mountains.'

So goes the story, however implausible. In reality the precise origin of the name is unknown but it dates from the early 19th century. In the Zulu language it is called, equally graphically, *uKhahlamba* – the Barrier of Spears.

It is a land of spectacular natural beauty; an extraordinary mountain range of huge peaks, towering basalt cliffs, massive sandstone outcrops, deep gorges and crystal-clear mountain streams. There is a good chance of seeing a variety of antelope and the area has a regular bird list of well over 200 species.

Add to this the fascinating history exemplified by the Bushman rock paintings spread widely across the whole area, together with its unique geological structure, and you can understand why it has been designated a World Heritage Site.

The Amphitheatre in the Royal Natal National Park seen from. The Sentinel is on the right.

The remote, high valley at Engagement Cave (Walk 69)

GEOGRAPHY

The Drakensberg mountains, which stretch from Cape Province up to Eastern Mpumalanga province, are the massive outer rim of the escarpment of the great interior plateau which is a major and climatically important feature of South Africa's topography. The Maloti-Drakensberg Park forms a crescent-shaped area 200km long, perched on the eastern border of Lesotho and stretching from the Royal Natal National Park (RNNP) in the north to the Sehlathebe NP of Lesotho in the south (see p30–31).

The escarpment itself and the plateau beyond are generally known as the High Berg, perhaps most famous for the 4km-wide sheer basalt wall of the Amphitheatre in the RNNP. The plateau has an average height of approximately 2900m, but numerous peaks reach much loftier altitudes. The highest point is the peak called Thaba Ntlenyama, lying inside Lesotho and at 3482m the highest point in Africa south of Kilimanjaro. There are many sheer rock walls of 500m or more. Below the High Berg is an area of numerous, lower, grass-covered mountains and smaller hills, known as the Little Berg, with its steep-sided spurs and valleys. The line of sandstone cliffs and outcrops that runs the entire length of the Drakensberg is a conspicuous feature and divides the Little Berg from the lower valleys.

GEOLOGY

Experts claim that the geology of the Drakensberg is 'simple'. Although that might well be the case for some people, less geologically aware souls such as the author struggle with the complexities of the subject. Fortunately even a basic understanding of the local geological history does a great deal to make the stunning scenery fall into historical perspective and adds to the pleasure of the walks.

From 250 to 300 million years ago the whole area was a vast expanse of shallow lakes, alluvial flats and swamps sitting on a large land-mass known as the super-continent of Gondwana: essentially today's Africa, South America, Antarctica, Australia and India. Flowing water separates particulate material according to size, so when gravel, sand, silt and mud were carried into the lake they were deposited in different places and layers upon underlying granite. This process, called sedimentation, continued over millions of years, and the weight of continuing deposits served to compact each underlying layer. This compaction formed what are known, unsurprisingly, as 'sedimentary rocks'. For example, sand accumulations are

converted into a sedimentary rock called sandstone, mud into mudstone (also called shale) and so on, although the names are not usually quite so obvious.

The lowest and therefore oldest layers that can be seen readily in the Drakensberg are those of the Molteno Formation, successive beds of sandstone alternating with layers of blue and grey mudstones. They often present a sparkling appearance because of the minute quartz crystals that bind together with sand particles. The most easily seen example is at Mermaid Pool in the Garden Castle area (see Walk 73).

The Elliot Formation, originally called 'Red Beds' because of the iron oxide content, has alternating layers of red mudstone and fine-grained sandstone. These are extensively exposed on the hillsides of the Drakensberg

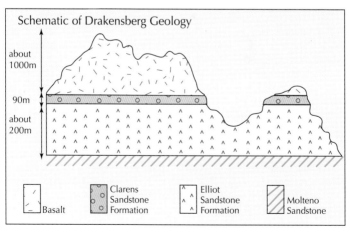

Schematic of Drakensberg Geology

about 1000m

90m

about 200m

Basalt

Clarens Sandstone Formation

Elliot Sandstone Formation

Molteno Sandstone

15

An outcrop of Clarens sandstone above the red-coloured Elliot Formation in Sleeping Beauty valley (Walk 69)

foothills and, when non-weathered, exhibit their characteristic dark red colouration.

Towards the end of this phase of sedimentation there was an increase in warming and aridity to produce desert conditions. The whole of today's South Africa, Zimbabwe, Botswana and Namibia became a vast sea of sand. The deposition that occurred at this time was wind rather than water-driven and these deposits formed the Clarens Formation. These huge sandstone cliffs cap many of the Drakensberg foothills, or Little Berg. They are often seen weathered into extraordinary shapes, a good example being Mushroom Rock in the Cathedral Peak area. In simple terms, winds have swirled across the rock face and picked up sand and other

particles which, in turn, have worn the cliff or rock away by an abrasive effect, forming caves.

This process is accentuated by surface water seeping down into cracks and subsequently freezing, thereby widening the cracks. The more this occurs, the more the likelihood of chunks of rock falling off as part of the erosion process, thus creating the beautiful and sometimes weird shapes seen in sandstone all over the area. Most of the caves in the area are found in this formation. The use of the word 'cave' is interesting: they are almost never true caves, more large overhangs.

For unknown reasons this period of sedimentation came to an abrupt end about 150 million years ago and subsequently the tectonic plates of

Gondwana started to drift apart. As well as breaking up Gondwana into the constituent continents that we recognise today, this stretched the plates and caused molten rock (magma) to burst through to the surface through a complex series of fissures or fractures in the earth's crust. The result was a succession of dramatic floods of basalt lava covering almost the whole of southern Africa. This gave rise to the layered appearance seen today, with individual lava flows of up to 20m in thickness.

In the area of the Drakensberg this solidified to a depth of at least 1000m especially over what is now Lesotho. The height of the cliffs and exposed steep slopes allowed subsequent weathering and erosion to bite into the margin of the lava plateau so that the broken material accumulated as an apron of rubble at the foot of the escarpment. In fact, of the extensive lava sheet that originally covered South Africa there are few such volcanic rock areas remaining in the region. The Drakensberg is probably the best place to see them and it is important to remember that the spectacular shapes of the peaks and rock formations are more the result of the later erosion by wind and water than by the original volcanic uplift. Generally, basalt cliffs are friable and make a poor playground for rock-climbers.

MAMMALS

There are 48 mammals recorded as living in the Drakensberg. Realistically you will see very few of

Basalt wall in the Sani Pass

them and if your aim is to see lots of mammals then you should plan on visiting a game reserve. But there is a good chance of seeing baboons, some antelope and dassies.

The Chacma sub-species of the Savanna Baboon

After man the baboon is the largest primate in southern Africa. Although very tolerant of different habitats they require cliffs or tall trees as a night-time refuge and must be near water. They are very gregarious and live in troops of anything from a dozen or so to a hundred or more. They are extremely vocal and it is baboons that are responsible for the angry barking that you will hear when walking in almost any area of the Drakensberg. You may find places where small rocks have been moved or overturned. This is a sign of baboons searching for invertebrates. You will also find shallow scrapings where they have looked for roots. Never feed them, never chase them and never corner them: they can be vicious. If they become habituated to feeding the Park Rangers will shoot them.

Antelope

Eland, Mountain Reedbuck, Grey Rhebok, Common Reedbuck, Oribi, Bushbuck, Blesbok, and Common Duiker are amongst the antelope that you may encounter in the Drakensberg. Of these, the first three are the most commonly seen.

Eland are the largest African antelope and occur naturally in the Drakensberg, the only place in southern South Africa where this is the case. Males may weigh up to 900kg, and although they are huge they can jump remarkable heights, easily clearing a 2m fence from a standing start. The herds are often large, 25 or more, but solitary animals and pairs are seen frequently.

The smaller your party and the less noise it makes, the better your chance of a good sighting. Very early in the morning is always the best time. As an aid to identification there are a number of books available with good photographs and clear descriptions.

Rock Dassie (Rock Hyrax)

Dassies look like rodents but are not. They are yellow-fawn in colour with paler underparts. Dassies are quite sociable and live in groups of up to about 40, they are rock dwellers and usually active after sunrise when they graze or browse. Their main predators are eagles. A giveaway sign of their dwellings is a white and brown streaked rock wall below the residence which is caused by the tidy disposal of 'waste' outside the hole.

Black-backed Jackal

The jackal is a canid (dog), widely seen across southern Africa and has a well demarcated black back flecked with white. The tail is black and bushy. They can be seen by day in reserves or other protected areas but are much more wary and nocturnal

Top *A watchful baboon*
Middle *Eland at Jacob's Ladder (Walk 53)*
Bottom *Rock dassies also climb trees*

Top *Blesbok*
Middle *Eland at Stromness Hill (Walk 65)*
Bottom *Feeding the baboons can have adverse consequences*

19

when threatened by the presence of man. They are usually seen as one of a pair or solitary. Their diet is very flexible and ranges from small or baby antelope, birds and rodents right down to berries and fruit. Jackals will kill goats, sheep or calves when the opportunity arises. Understandably this antagonises the farming community who, with good reason, regard them as pests.

Leopard

This magnificent animal is uncommon but widely distributed in the Drakensberg. It is rarely seen: not for nothing is it described as 'the Prince of Stealth'. Powerfully built and amazingly catholic in its dietary habits, it lives in woodland and rocky outcrops and is included here because it is the only large predator in the Park. It poses no risk to walkers.

Although not in the cat family, it is of interest that both spotted and brown hyaena have been captured recently on camera traps but sightings are very rare.

SNAKES

There are a lot of snakes in Africa, some 170 species in southern Africa alone. However, tourists rarely see one and, if they do, it is unlikely to be venomous. More people in South Africa are killed by lightning than by snakes. The Berg does have its share of snakes and it is prudent to know something about them, in particular,

what to do in the highly unlikely event of an 'incident'. Visitors in the high summer months of December, January and February are the most likely to see a snake. By April they are preparing to hibernate and so may still be moving around looking for that last precious calorie for storage. It is more unusual to see one in May but by September they're back.

The three snakes described here are the only significantly venomous ones you might encounter.

Puff Adder *(Bitis arietans)*

Most snakes detect your approach by their highly-developed vibratory sense and make their escape before you see them. One exception is the Puff Adder, a slow-moving and bad-tempered piece of work who likes to bask in the sun and freezes rather than moving away, anticipating that excellent camouflage will save the day. It is a stout snake, yellow-brown in colour with black chevrons and a triangular head quite distinct from the body, some 90cm in length on average but sometimes much longer. Its venom is very potent and cytotoxic (cell destroying), and envenomation is serious. Death is rare but the bite, from the snake's very large fangs, is hugely painful and tissue damage may occur, often severe enough to require grafting or even the loss of part of a limb. This snake is responsible for about 60 per cent of all serious snake bites in South Africa. It is rarely found above 2000m altitude.

Puff Adder

Berg Adder *(Bitis atropos)*
As the name suggests this is predominantly found on high-altitude rocky slopes and mountain grassland and is the most common Drakensberg snake. It is similar in appearance

Rinkhals – a spitting snake

to the Puff Adder but less brightly coloured, without the chevrons, and much smaller, averaging 30cm and sometimes just 10–20cm. As bad-tempered as the Puff Adder, possibly even more so, it hisses loudly and strikes readily but tends to seek refuge much more quickly. Unusually for an adder it has a mildly neurotoxic venom (that is, affecting the nervous system) and specifically has an effect on the nerves controlling the muscles of the face and tongue. This manifests itself as drooping eyelids, double vision, dizziness and sometimes difficulty in swallowing. This is all very alarming but no deaths have been reported.

Rinkhals *(Hemachatus haemachatus)*
This is a bigger snake than the previous three, averaging more than 1m in length and similar to a cobra in appearance (but it isn't one),

21

spreading a 'hood' when threatened. In the Drakensberg it is often banded black and yellow or black and deep orange, with two or three distinct white bars on its chest only seen when it raises itself vertically from the ground which it does as a defensive posture. This is a scary moment. However, generally it tries to escape when disturbed. Like most cobras it has neurotoxic venom and its bite must be considered serious.

It is unusual in two respects. Firstly it is a 'spitting' snake and can project venom for up to 3m very accurately towards the eyes. This is only harmful if it actually gets into the eyes, so keep well clear (see 'Immediate Action' box, p40). Secondly, it has a defensive tactic of playing dead (thanatosis), mouth often open with tongue hanging out. Don't be fooled: it can be very convincing. Move away and never pick up apparently deceased serpents.

BIRDS

The Drakensberg has an extensive bird list, often quoted as over 300 species. However, this includes vagrants and some birds that are only very rarely seen. Realistically, if any visitor ticks more than 200 species in the Drakensberg then she or he is doing well. For committed birders there are a number of 'Drakensberg specials', that is, species that are more easily seen here than elsewhere. At lower altitudes you will see a lot of

birds wherever you walk, but fewer in autumn and winter than in spring and summer.

Apart from the ubiquitous Cape Sparrows and Southern Grey-headed Sparrows you will see particularly Greater Double-collared Sunbirds, Red-winged Starlings, Cape Whiteeyes, White-necked Ravens, Hadeda Ibis and various doves almost everywhere. Many will find a bird identification book indispensable.

Bearded Vulture

Originally known as the Lammergeier, this is the most famous bird of the Drakensberg. There may only be 60 breeding pairs remaining. Here and neighbouring Lesotho are the only sites in South Africa where it can be seen.

If you're close the identification is straightforward. The black wings, orange-brown neck, underparts and legs, yellow eyes and red eye-ring are characteristic. The 'beard' is more of a black, drooping feathered moustache. In flight from underneath note the rich orange-brown underparts, black pointed wings and long, black, wedge-shaped tail. The birds feed on carrion which they drop repeatedly from a height onto rocks to break up the bones with their constituent marrow.

This is a great and rare bird to see. A major conservation effort sponsored by KZN Wildlife is in place, which encourages observers to report sightings. (A copy of their promotional poster is reproduced with their permission on page 24.)

Above *The frequently seen Greater Double-collared Sunbird*

Left *The endangered Bearded Vulture*

Bottom left *Jackal Buzzard on the Sani Pass*

Below *The South African endemic Ground Woodpecker living up to its name*

WANTED:
THE BEARDED VULTURE

We require your assistance in the sighting of marked Bearded Vultures

The Bearded Vulture is an endangered species occurring in the Maloti-Drakensberg mountains. Their numbers are continually declining as a result of several threats including: a shortage of the right type of food, poisonings and collisions with powerlines.

KZN Wildlife is monitoring the Bearded Vulture population to obtain more information on where these birds feed, roost and nest. This information will highlight potential threats that need to be addressed to save the species from extinction. We have marked a few birds by bleaching their wing feathers and now need your help in finding these marked birds!

How can YOU help?

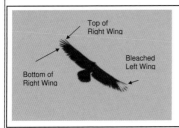

Top of Right Wing

Bleached Left Wing

Bottom of Right Wing

If you see a marked bird, record and send in the following information:

- Date
- Time
- Location
- Which wing is bleached
- Whether the top or bottom feathers of the wing were bleached *(e.g. the top of the bird's left wing is bleached in the photograph on the left)*
- Take a photograph if possible

The Bearded Vulture (left) could be confused with the Black Eagle (middle) or the Cape Vulture (right). See the differences between the underwing and the shape of the tail of the birds below.

BEARDED VULTURE
Adult bird with diamond shaped tail. Juveniles are dark in colour.

BLACK EAGLE
Adult bird with white markings on both wings. Juvenile is brown.

CAPE VULTURE
Larger bird with pale body and dark edges on wings and tail.

Please report information to gypaetus@kznwildlife.com or Sonja Krüger of *Ezemvelo* KZN Wildlife at + 27 33 239 1514.

Glossy Berg Bottlebrush (Greyia sutherlandii) – a small tree with beautiful flowers on high rocky slopes

THE HABITATS

Fortunately, most of the original Drakensberg habitat hasn't changed significantly over the years, except in respect of the composition of some of the grassland. What you see today is to a large extent what was there a long time ago.

Grassland, rich in flowering plants, accounts for more than half of the area. This is important in the maintenance of a stable population of antelope, and for the birds, large and small, who favour this habitat. Their specific distribution is dictated by the height of the grass, so diversity is crucial.

Patches of woodland, including scrub, are scattered throughout, especially, but not invariably, close to watercourses. There is little grass within woodland, which reduces the risk of fire damage. This is also a bird-rich environment. The wooded areas as well as the cliffs are the domain of the troops of Savanna Baboons which every walker will see or at least hear.

The Drakensberg is studded with streams, but there are no true wetlands because of the excellent drainage of the steep ground. Streams are usually fast-flowing because of the gradient, with pools, waterfalls and steep rock walls. Some specialised flora cling precariously to these walls and flourish there. This is the home of the Cape Clawless Otter, the Drakensberg being its best-known territory. You may notice its scat, studded with white crustacean shell fragments, but to see the animal itself a dawn start and some luck are required.

Gurney's Sugarbird

*Wild Dagga (Leonotis leonurus),
much-favoured by Malachite sunbirds*

Everywhere you look you see rocky outcrops. Where they occur on grassland slopes they make for a small ecosystem of their own. They act as a safe haven for a number of specialist plants. The widespread Rock Dassie lives here and it is the haunt of some specialised birds, including the Ground Woodpecker. At higher altitudes you may see the colourful and endemic Drakensberg Crag Lizard sunning itself on warm boulders.

Some visitors are disappointed in the Drakensberg when they visit in spring and do not see it alive with colourful flowers. This is particularly true if they compare it with the magnificent floral wealth of, say, the Western Cape. But the Drakensberg is almost unique in its geology, site and particularly altitude, which makes for difficult comparisons. Also, the area is dominated by extensive grassland and flowers are often difficult to see. Nevertheless, the altitude rises from 1280m to almost 3500m so there is an opportunity to see a rich variety of plant life. With well over 2000 species of plants recorded, over 300 of which are endemic to the area, it is not exactly a desert.

The hallmark genus of the Drakensberg for many tourists is the Protea with its six local species. There can be no finer sight than a mountain hillside covered with flowering Protea. The Common Tree Fern (Cyathea dregei) is relatively easy to see in many areas, but in others it has become extinct after being extensively pillaged for planting in gardens. It is now protected by law. Up to 5m in height with a crown of arching fronds, it tends to be found in full sun, especially in gullies with a stream close by.

Fire as an ecological tool

When walking in the Drakensberg you will frequently come across areas of burnt grassland. It can look awful. There are three principal causes of fire: lightning, arson and planned burns.

The use of fire in grassland management is long-established and, when used appropriately, of proven scientific value. It removes dead organic material in the winter (the dry season) and prevents or removes encroachment by undesirable plants. In the Drakensberg the main aim is to maintain or develop

A firebreak seen from the summit of Sterkhorn (Walk 32)

grass cover for soil and water conservation. Firebreak creation is an important concomitant strategy for limiting the spread of natural or deliberate fires. The creation of firebreaks is a skilled business needing much care and a lot of tough work. Indeed, originally it was done with a hoe!

These burns are usually carried out on a two or three-year cyclical basis. When walking in April to June or early July it is important to check where planned burns are taking place and stay clear of these areas. The information should be available at the KZNW local office.

Major planned grass burn at Cobham

GETTING CLEAR OF A FIRE

In the unlikely event of encountering such a fire at close quarters (a very alarming experience) remember that you cannot outrun it. There may be a stream or other watery haven close at hand. But if a fire comes towards you and escape looks difficult, light the grass around you and follow the line of flames downwind so that you are in a 'grass-free zone'. If you can control the fire so much the better but it may be impossible. Always carry a box of matches or a lighter in the dry season.

What are the risks to plants and animals? Fire rarely kills trees, grass growth is enhanced and some plants, for example *Protea caffra*, require the smoke to stimulate dormant seeds. Bigger animals can make good their escape and most smaller ones survive in burrows. Some insects succumb but then act as a food supply for birds.

BUSHMAN PAINTINGS

The first evidence of human occupation of the Drakensberg Park area dates back to the Middle Stone Age, some 20,000 years ago. The Bushmen (or San people) were classical hunter-gatherers and decorated caves or rock overhangs with paintings now sometimes known as rock art. They did not necessarily use these places as habitation. The practice started at least 2000 years ago and finished when the last of them had disappeared in the 20th century, mostly by deliberate pursuit and murder. It is said that there are about 20,000 individual rock paintings and engravings spread over more than 500 sites of caves and overhangs.

Important examples have been declared as national monuments including Giant's Castle Main Caves, Game Pass shelter in the Kamberg Nature Reserve and Battle Cave in the Injisuthi valley. These centres offer guided walks to paintings. The Kamberg Reserve also has a good Interpretation Centre as does Didima camp at Cathedral Peak. There are many other sites of fine quality that have not been so honoured and some, notably those in the Didima valley, are currently closed to the public.

Some paintings are monochromatic but others use two colours or more and are very realistic. The colours used tend to be limited to red, brown, yellow, black and white because of the available materials. Paintings in black and white are more likely to have deteriorated or disappeared, so most of those remaining are of the yellow–red–brown spectrum. Binding substances were required to blend the colours and the whole process was exceedingly complex. Bones, sticks or fingers were used to apply the paints.

The hugely significant Rosetta Panel at Game Pass Shelter, showing a dying Eland with a therianthrope (half human/half animal) holding its tail

The ideas behind this art are more complex than hitherto imagined. Originally it was assumed that the paintings were a simple representation of lifestyle and life events. More recently it has been proposed that much of the art had a spiritual implication, particularly as many depict half-man, half-animal figures. The artists might be both paying homage to animals on which their life depended (such as Eland, the most commonly depicted) and attempting, through art,

Above *During a trance shamans had an altered state of consciousness and experienced sensations such as an extended scalp or spiritual energy leaving their heads*

Left *This could be interpreted literally as people running away from a leopard, or as imagery – the leopard is often associated with shamans, intermediaries between the human and the spirit world*

29

to harness their power. Nevertheless, it is clear that historical narration also played a part, with some of the paintings, showing wagons drawn by oxen and men on horseback, clearly relating to the arrival of white settlers in the area.

The work was accomplished by certain key individuals, the 'Shamans', rather than all members of a social group. These individuals bridged the chasm between the spiritual and the real world. Trance, possibly induced by hallucinogenics on occasion, was important prior to completion.

There are several threats to the rock art of the Drakensberg. The principal ones are natural weathering of the paint (and of the rock) and, sadly, vandalism. The rock shelters were originally created by the process of weathering and it is just a continuation of this process that is causing the damage. How this might be reduced is the subject of much research. Fires lit by people camping in the shelters have created smoke damage and some visitors have even wet the paintings to improve the colours – if they used carbonated drinks to do this the damage is even more significant. A number of initiatives have been taken including forbidding camping in painted caves, fencing some areas off and eliminating the marking of caves on maps.

Access to Bushman painting sites is permitted only if accompanied by one of the widely available qualified and registered guides. I have been advised that it would be imprudent to define exactly the location of where paintings can be seen on routes in this book except where it is clearly a walk to a formally guided site. Nevertheless, when walking in any of the areas, especially in the southern Drakensberg, be alert for that moment when your route takes you slap bang into some paintings. Look particularly at the walls of large overhangs. If you chance upon some paintings be sure to treat them reverently and touch them not.

THE DEVELOPMENT OF THE PARK

The history of the Drakensberg Park goes back a long way. In October 1903 the Natal Colony government took the first step towards its establishment with a Government Notice which stated its intention to create a 'game reserve on the Crown land in the vicinity of Giant's Castle'. Next came the establishment of the Natal National Park in 1916, the prefix 'Royal' being added after a visit by the British Royal family in 1947. Gradually more and more areas were designated as protected by the purchase of farmland and by the late 1960s the park was more or less what it is today. Altogether it comprises 242,813 hectares (almost 2500km2) and is the largest mountain wilderness area in Africa. The official title 'the uKhahlamba-Drakensberg Park' was introduced in 2000, but for brevity the

Subsistence farming community outside Lotheni

terms 'the Drakensberg', 'the Park', and 'the Berg' will be used interchangeably throughout this book.

More recently, the uKhahlamba-Drakensberg Park has been subsumed within the Maloti-Drakensberg Transboundary World Heritage Site, amalgamating with the Sehlathabe NP of Lesotho. Accordingly, the Drakensberg Parks are now labelled with the name 'Maloti-Drakensberg Park' and this is used thoughout the book.

Ezemvelo KwaZulu-Natal Wildlife (EZKZNW, commonly referred to as KZN Wildlife or KZNW) is the conservation management agency in the province of KwaZulu-Natal and is responsible for the South African part of the enlarged Park.

Apart from its headline roles of assuring sustainable use of the Park's biodiversity and wildlife conservation, KZN Wildlife has a pivotal role in the development of ecotourism. The Drakensberg Park is almost entirely surrounded by farmland. There are large cattle farms but local community subsistence farming predominates. Amongst these local communities there is significant unemployment. Ecotourism carries with it the responsibility of involving these communities.

KZNW has created many jobs, particularly through its participation in the 'Work for Water' scheme introduced in 1995. It is well known that trees deplete the water supply, and when these trees are alien plants (Black Wattle – *Acacia mearnsii*, and species of Eucalyptus, especially *E saligna*, are a particular problem) the pressure to remove them becomes intense. The Work for Water initiative has vigorously addressed this problem and at the same time helped to alleviate some of the poverty. Tourism plays its part in increasing employment by the opening

31

An armed KZNW Ranger on patrol

of camps and hotels, and also provides opportunities for Community Guides. These are local people trained to guide walks and, most importantly, conduct visitors to sites of Bushman paintings.

Finally, it is important to mention KZNW involvement, in co-operation with the South African Police Service, in anti-smuggling operations to interrupt the marijuana (locally known as 'dagga') trade from Lesotho.

While tourism has always been encouraged and is now an important part of the economic development of communities bordering the Park, it would be wrong to underestimate the problems that ensue. These include resort development and its knock-on effects and, sadly, physical damage to cave paintings. Examples of future development might include cable cars, hotels on the plateau and skiing as well as the ever-present threat of private housing schemes. Walkers will not see this as advantageous and there is certainly a lobby that feels that

this will put unreasonable pressure on an already vulnerable ecosystem. Personally, my recommendation is to visit the Park before further significant development takes place, however eco-friendly that might be.

ABOUT THE WALKS

It should be said at the outset that no walks in the Drakensberg Park should be underestimated. The unpredictability of the weather is legendary and the terrain often difficult. Local advice is available and should be sought if there is any doubt about the feasibility of a particular route for your party.

The walks described here are grouped by geographical area from north to south. Each geographical section of the Drakensberg seems to have its own character, a certain 'feel' as you arrive, but it is a difficult concept to describe. So, although the Park is often and reasonably heralded as a single entity based on the obvious topographical features of the escarpment and the Little Berg, each part is in reality quite different from the next, with its own unique flavour and attraction.

The **Contour Path** is an important concept to grasp. It is, more or less, what it sounds like; a path following the contour as best it can across the whole of the area under discussion. Presently it runs almost completely from the Cathedral Peak area right down to Bushman's Nek at the extreme south of the Drakensberg Park. But, and it is a big but, anyone who thinks

Sleeping Beauty Valley –
Magnificent Valley leads
off to the right (Walk 69)

that this infers a nice level path which is invariably easy to follow should think again. It is often extremely undulating, can be very rough underfoot and, on occasion, tricky to follow. Nevertheless, it does have a useful, sometimes pivotal, link role when creating round-trip day-long walks and is also a handy tool in route description.

By virtue of their inclusion in this book all the walks are recommended. What makes one route better than another? Inevitably it is in the eye of the beholder and involves a number of parameters including scenery, botanical interest, bird life, rivers to play in and many other factors; often it is not even precisely definable. So, personal preferences notwithstanding, there's no star system or similar here.

Route selection

All guidebooks have limitations of space. This means that route selection is inevitable and some areas with good potential for walking may need to be excluded completely. **Mnweni** is an inhabited grazing and farming area which is not within the Park proper, lying immediately south of the RNNP. Although some aspects of the area are certainly improving, there is a lack of accommodation and facilities generally and tourism is currently limited. **Mkhomazi** KZN Wildlife Office entrance to the Park has reasonable access from the Nottingham Road area but no facilities or campsite and, although it has superb, remote walking country available, has little to offer the confirmed day walker. Similarly **Vergelegen**, which has its own access distance issue, has no facilities and many of the paths are overgrown. Certainly it is a great start point for longer forays into the High Berg but day visitors rarely go there.

33

Local Zulu craft worker

The Drakensberg is an area with massive potential for walking and is South Africa's most popular walking area. Backpacking with appropriate gear including food, a stove, sleeping bag, and a tent or a cave for overhead cover extends horizons considerably. However, of the visitors to the Park, the majority plan on returning to their base accommodation before nightfall. This applies particularly to foreign visitors who are unable to bring equipment on the scale required within the constraints of airline baggage allowances, and who may not wish to locate, hire and then collect equipment after arrival, or do not wish to hire a guide with equipment.

This book is aimed specifically at those who wish to do walks that can be completed in a day. There is something here for families with small children, as well as intermediate walks and some much tougher challenges.

GETTING THERE

Access to South Africa by air is currently almost entirely through Johannesburg. Most European long-haul carriers fly there directly (including British Airways and Virgin Atlantic from London Heathrow) as does South African Airways. There is an Emirates flight from Dubai directly to Durban and Turkish Airlines fly there from Istanbul. The routes have become quite competitive and it is well worth using an agent or the Internet to seek out the best fare, even if it means a change of flight in a European city. From the United States there are non-stop flights to Johannesburg with Delta (Atlanta) and South African Airways (JFK, New York) plus a direct flight with South African (IAD, Washington) with a refuelling stop in Accra.

Visitors from the EU and Switzerland do not require a visa

to enter South Africa. Residents of other countries should check at www. home-affairs.gov.za.

There is no public transport to carry you into the Drakensberg so self-drive is the only reasonable possibility. There are many car hire companies located in the airports.

Almost everyone gets to the area from or via Johannesburg or Durban. From other locations the main axis of the N3 toll road still applies unless you design your own cross-country route. Although 'N' roads may have central barriers and slip-road exits there are important differences from European motorways. Pedestrians are frequently seen, there is some hitch-hiking, livestock may wander onto the road and petrol stations can be relatively long distances apart. There is a series of small towns, some a little way off the N3, which are recognised 'feeders' for the Drakensberg and where you can refuel and pick up supplies, especially important if you are self-catering.

A good route-planning road map is important for identifying the shortest or the most interesting way of getting to your destination in the Drakensberg once you leave the N3. Many by-roads are unsurfaced, can be very rough and in wet weather may make for challenging driving conditions. Even surfaced roads may have huge potholes.

From Johannesburg

Leaving OR Tambo International Airport you exit on R24 which joins

Even surfaced roads need vigilance

the N12 briefly before you take the slip road L onto the N3. This road and its southern destination of Durban are well signposted. It may be busy and slow at rush-hour times but is navigationally simple. The first key town is Harrismith, about 3hrs steady driving from the airport. From then on the relevant exits and some associated notes are shown under the headings of the individual Park sections. Generally the signposting from the N3 is satisfactory.

From Durban

King Shaka International is the airport for Durban and is sited at La Mercy, some 30km north of the centre of the city. There is a connection from the airport to the N2, the north–south main coastal road. Drive south and after about 30km join the N3 at a large interchange, following signs for Pietermaritzburg which is about 80km distant.

Soon after Pietermaritzburg opportunities arise to leave the N3 axis to make your way into the

Drakensberg area of your choice. These are detailed in the information box at the beginning of each geographical section. Wherever you are heading, Durban is closer than Johannesburg, sometimes substantially.

FUEL, CASH AND PERMITS

Some hotels and some of the camps in the Park have petrol supplies but this can be unreliable. So it is wise to fill up before you leave the N3 or in one of the feeder towns.

Some B&Bs, park entrances and local guides only take cash payments. This means carrying a significant sum with you as driving back to an ATM will be time-consuming and expensive.

You will need R40 per person per day (2016 price) for your mandatory park permit though rates may vary from area to area. They are available from the park entrance gates during normal working hours (usually 8am to 4pm, often closed for lunch).

ACCOMMODATION

Many parts of the Drakensberg are comparatively remote. Given that some areas have little choice of accommodation it is very important to secure this in advance to obviate a wasted, long and possibly awkward drive. This is particularly relevant in the case of the KZN-Wildlife rest camps, often fully booked many months in advance.

The South African peak holiday times are Easter, most of December and the first half of January. Bookings can be made by telephone, especially from South Africa, although it is also increasingly possible to book over the internet.

In the sections of the book which cover the individual geographical areas of the Drakensberg some indication is given as to whether accommodation is plentiful or sparse together with some recommendations from the author's personal experience (although standards may change from year to year).

Some of these accommodation details, including general websites which contain information on hotels, bed-and-breakfast establishments, rest camps and so on, are listed in Appendix C, together with telephone numbers where available. Nevertheless, there is no real substitute for doing your own research because it is more fun and brings to your attention all sorts of other interesting stuff.

THE CLIMATE – WHEN TO VISIT

The Drakensberg has summers with hot days and refreshingly cool evenings but accompanied by high rainfall, often with thunderstorms which can be frighteningly dramatic. The maximum temperature in the valleys is around 35°C. In summer cloud cover is very common on the summits.

Winters can be very cold, especially at high altitude. At night on the

A spring day at Cobham – snow can occur at any time of year

summit plateau the temperature may be as low as -20°C. Although, frost occurs frequently and heavy snow is possible,the overall precipitation in winter accounts for less than ten per cent of the annual total.

It is difficult to recommend a 'best time' for visitors who want to walk in the Drakensberg. April and May are usually excellent with reasonable daytime temperatures but cool nights and, importantly, blue skies with low average rainfall, but this is not absolutely reliable. The downside of May and June is that there may be some haze related to the burning programmes (see 'The Habitats' above) but this really only interferes with photography. September is often a good month with all the signs of emerging spring, and daytime temperatures rising nicely. The higher rainfall season is just beginning at that stage.

Temperatures by month
Cathedral Peak Hotel (1470m)

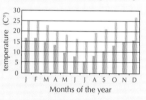

low ▓ high
By kind permission of Cathedral Peak Hotel

Average rainfall
Royal Natal National Park

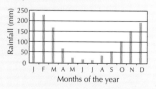

37

From mid-October to March rainfall is quite high, and manifest especially as heavy thunderstorms in the afternoon. So to a certain extent it depends why you are visiting the Drakensberg. For long hikes, the end of April, May and possibly June or September are excellent. In summer they are still possible but a very early start is required. For flowers and birds November and December have much to offer.

The important underlying message is that temperature, rainfall and wind are, notwithstanding charts showing averages, unpredictable. Sudden changes in the weather are notorious. The bottom line is that whenever you visit you should be prepared for almost any conditions at any time.

HEALTH MATTERS

Malaria

There is no risk of malaria in the Drakensberg.

Gastrointestinal infections

All travellers recognise that there is a risk of gut infection when travelling abroad. When there is any question of contaminated supplies, simple precautions such as avoiding fruit that you can't peel and drinking bottled water or other drinks will minimise problems.

In the Drakensberg the question of whether or not to drink from mountain streams is an important one. If there is human habitation upstream it should be absolutely ruled out. If there is Baboon habitation upstream

Royal Natal National Park – visibility on the plateau can be limited for days at a time

Most walkers drink safely from streams

the risk is uncertain but probably remote. Some infections can, however, be passed from animals to humans through water supplies so the risk, however small, does exist.

Medical authorities often advise against drinking from streams. However, generations of South African hikers (and the author) have partaken of delicious, cold and sometimes very necessary refreshment from this source without harm. You must decide.

Dealing with snake bites

Some common-sense practical steps considerably lessen the risk of significant snakebite. Wearing proper walking boots and thick socks in the Berg provides some defence against an inadvertent step onto a basking snake, and gaiters add a little more protection. Don't put your hands under logs or masonry and never into

holes in the ground, especially in old termite mounds. And never, ever, pick up snakes even if you think you recognise their harmlessness, unless you are a real expert.

Most venomous snakes can control whether or not they inject venom in a bite and if so in what volume. Therefore, to be bitten by a venomous snake may not be associated with envenomation and symptoms. The circumstance where no venom is injected is known as a 'dry bite'. If the snake delivering the bite has been recognised all well and good but do not try and follow it with intent to kill on the basis of information gathering or revenge. This tactic may lead to a doubling of casualty numbers.

Symptoms

Generally the earliest symptoms after snakebite are those of anxiety related to fear of the consequences. These may include dryness of the mouth, sweating and tachycardia (fast heart rate) with nausea. With cytotoxic venom there is immediate and severe burning pain at the site of the bite and then local swelling which may continue for two to three days.

After neurotoxic envenomation there may be local pain but little or no swelling, with drowsiness, vomiting and increased sweating within five to 30 minutes. Later, from 30 minutes to three hours, more obvious nervous system effects emerge which may lead ultimately to difficulty with swallowing or breathing.

First aid management

The victim needs to get to an appropriately-equipped medical unit as soon as possible. This may be difficult. Fortunately, you will usually have sufficient time accomplish this and it has been reckoned that even without any first-aid or formal medical treatment at least 98 per cent of snakebite victims survive.

However, **all walkers in the Drakensberg should have a sound knowledge of basic First Aid including CPR**. Some areas are very remote and accidents happen.

So what steps can you take and should you not take in preparation for evacuation?

Immediate action
✓ Keep calm
✓ Get help whenever possible. There may be a mobile phone signal. It may be necessary to send someone for help.

Things you SHOULD do
✓ Keep the victim still and calm. Reassurance is an important management tool and it is always worth reminding those bitten that most recover completely without any treatment. (They won't believe you if you are panicking yourself.) Unnecessary movement may hasten the spread of venom.
✓ Expose the wound and wipe away excess venom
✓ Remove tight clothing, jewellery and shoes
✓ Immobilise the affected limb
✓ Be prepared to give CPR if any sign of difficulty in breathing
✓ If the snake has successfully projected venom into the eyes, rinse the eyes out with, ideally, running water. Alternatives are milk, beer, other cold drinks or urine.

Things you should NOT do
✗ Do not cut, squeeze or suck the bite
✗ Do not give an electric shock to the bite – there is no evidence of efficacy
✗ Do not give alcohol
✗ Do not administer antivenom – indeed don't carry any!

Download onto your cellphone the free app 'Snakebite First Aid', devised by the African Snakebite Institute. Then read it.

Dehydration
Even at some of the modest temperatures experienced in the Berg, slog-
ging up hills with a rucksack induces
considerable water loss. Most people
don't replenish this sufficiently and
feel at least uncomfortable and, at
worst, increasingly tired and weak
before they realise their plight.
Carrying enough water for your needs
is tough because of the weight penalty
but is absolutely essential. At least two
litres a day is a minimum for all but
the shortest outings.

Altitude problems
Although the altitudes are never
extreme many people will find the
going tougher if they are unaccus-
tomed to walking above, say, 2000m.
In particular, driving up the Sani Pass
to then climb Hodgson's Peaks will
be sufficient to give most people a
sharp reminder that they will need to
reduce their normal speed of march.
Dehydration is more of an issue too if
you're working harder.

Immunisation
Well before departure consult your
family doctor, from whom current
national advice will be available. It
should go without saying that unpro-
tected sex might have extremely serious consequences.

Health insurance
This is absolutely mandatory when
you go anywhere outside your own
country, unless you have unlimited

capital and are unconcerned about
parting with a large amount of it. It
is worthwhile reading the small print
most assiduously. Pay particular attention to anything related to restrictions
on the terrain that is covered by the
policy and anything involving mountain rescue.

Health care in South Africa
Standards of health care in South
Africa can be as high as anywhere in
the world and this applies particularly
in the larger cities. In very rural communities the facilities and specialist
expertise available are less predictable. Generally, the concept of trans-
fering problem cases to a larger and
better-equipped unit is well accepted,
but distances are long and some minor
roads are poorly surfaced, rendering
transfer times longer than anticipated
if air transport is unavailable.

SAFETY

Mountain rescue
Entry permits for the Maloti-
Drakensberg Park are mandatory. This
includes a component to cover you in
the event of rescue being required.

Optimum group size
Most authorities recommend three or
four as the minimum number, especially for travel up on the escarpment:
at least one to stay with a casualty,
at least one to run for help if necessary. For the purposes of walks in this
book the same number applies, but

in practice, up to and including the Contour Path, many pairs of walkers are encountered. In good weather most people find that acceptable. The difficult question is whether one should walk alone? There is no simple answer to this as there are so many variable factors involved, but if a lone walk is your preference and decision, it is absolutely essential that route and estimated return time are recorded at a place where it will checked later.

It is interesting to note that, although it is a bounden duty for all walkers to act responsibly and reduce to a minimum the chance of needing to call out a rescue party, the Drakensberg Park authorities continue to stress that you, the walker, have a 'Right to Risk'. Many will find this a refreshing attitude.

SECURITY

Sadly, at the time of writing South Africa carries a reputation for increasing lawlessness. Car-jacking is relatively common and mugging, as in the UK, frequently reported in urban areas. However, most tourists never experience any security problems and preventative measures are broadly similar to those that many take in their own country.

Within the Drakensberg Park it is highly unusual for significant incidents to occur which involve tourists. Lone walkers are not uncommon and pairs more common than any other group in our experience. There are prominent warnings about avoiding contact wherever possible with Basutho traders and smugglers (often of marijuana, locally called 'dagga') who may also do some stock rustling

THINGS TO CONSIDER FOR MAXIMUM SECURITY

- Do not leave very valuable or important items in an unattended car even if they are well concealed. Never leave passport, credit cards or money.
- If you have the misfortune to have a puncture try keep an eye on your luggage. Offers of assistance are common and usually friendly and supportive but a gratuity is welcomed so have some coins at hand.
- It is generally agreed that it is inadvisable to travel by road in the countryside, even on major roads, at night.
- In hotels use the room safe if there is one or hotel security if there is not. Don't leave precious items in plain view. It may offer temptation to low-paid people and is unfair on them if you mislay an item and presume it stolen.
- In the street don't flash wads of banknotes, expensive jewellery or electronics that might attract would-be-muggers.

Completing the mountain register is vital

on the side. If you encounter them on the path move aside. It is reasonable to acknowledge their presence with a polite wave or a 'hello' but don't engage with them and never take photographs or ask to see what's in their sacks. It is sensible to ask for local advice about this aspect of safety wherever you are.

Useful telephone numbers

Consider putting key telephone numbers (see Appendix C) in the contact list of your mobile telephone (cellphone). Add the number of your accommodation as well and, possibly, your insurer's number and airline office contact. Always make clear which number is the Emergency Contact number for your next of kin.

COMMUNICATIONS

Apart from hotels, generally in South Africa the mobile phone (cellphone) is king and has quite good coverage, although in the mountains this is much less predictable.

Some KZNW camps have a good signal but once out in the Berg the most reliable reception areas are on ridges or summits. In respect of safety you should assume lack of signal. For visitors from abroad, to reduce costs consider taking an old phone with you and purchasing both SIM and airtime on arrival.

In case of serious issues arising on your walk, ensure you have the numbers of your accommodation, the police and the KZN Wildlife emergency service (ask at the local office) nestling in your contact list.

Wifi availability is poor away from hotels and some cafés. In my experience only a few B&Bs and KZN Wildlife lodges offer internet connectivity. Visitors usually have to rely on 3G for Internet access.

MAPS

For walking maps of the Drakensberg there is a series at 1:50,000 scale published by KZN Wildlife and last revised in 2003. In this book they are referred to as KZNW maps. The geographical areas covered by the six available maps are as follows (with some overlap):

* Hiking Map 1
  Royal Natal National Park
* Hiking Map 2
  Cathedral Peak and Monk's Cowl
* Hiking Map 3
  Giant's Castle and Injisuthi
* Hiking Map 4
  Highmoor and Kamberg

43

Chain ladders can deteriorate. Ask about them beforehand (Walk 7)

- Hiking Map 5
  Cobham and Lotheni
- Hiking Map 6
  Garden Castle and Bushman's
  Nek

The 1:50,000 scale is acceptable for walking trips in this area. Unfortunately this Drakensberg series has limitations in that some paths and other features are incorrectly plotted, sometimes significantly so in navigational terms. Later editions of the maps may correct inaccuracies. Note that in the current edition all references to caves with Bushman paintings have been excluded to reduce the possibility of vandalism.

The routes in this guide are accompanied by sketch maps. Red dashed lines are used to illustrate routes that have been walked and validated. Red dotted lines are either alternatives that have been explored (indicated on the sketch) or just other paths you may encounter.

Maps are drawn to scale and based on GPS-derived information but they are just sketches and should be used in conjunction with the appropriate map. A map and compass should be regarded as essential equipment.

USING THIS GUIDE

Route gradings

The difficulty of grading walking routes is widely recognised. One man's stroll along a narrow ridge, hands in pockets, is another's worst nightmare. Many factors are involved, including weather, fitness and confidence as well as the experience and opinions of the reporter.

For these reasons a simple system has been adopted which should give an indication of whether a route is for you. The statistics quoted for each route include the total distance for the route (round trip or there and back) and an estimate of the height gained. These were recorded by GPS.

	Distance	Ascent
Easy	< 11km	< 400m
Moderate	11–20km	401–1000m
Strenuous	20km +	1000m +

In addition, any circumstances which might complicate the route are also indicated in brackets after the grading, where necessary. These are:
- exposure (E)
- chain ladders (L) – usually vertical or near-vertical and so daunting for some, and
- route-finding issues (or trackless terrain) (T).

Routes where a rope is essential are outside the scope of this book.

The only abbreviations used in route descriptions are SP (signpost), L and R (left and right), and N, S, E, W (north, south, east and west).

Route timings

Timing routes is a traditionally awkward task. Fitness and pack weight, for example, vary between and within individuals. Some days are

The extremely steep cleft of the Mudslide, to the left of the central buttress (Walk 4)

just bad days. In this guide the walking times were recorded conventionally with a watch and included stops for drinks, photographs, calls of nature and so on but excluded meal or picnic halts. They are recorded as total there-and-back times. It is certain that our overall speed varied from day-to-day, especially as personnel also changed, so these are very much guide times. After a couple of routes it should be possible to extrapolate the book timings to your times and make appropriate adjustments to your planning. To use a golfing analogy, there is no such thing as a par time and certainly no bonus for a birdie.

THE GIANT'S CUP TRAIL

The Giant's Cup Trail is a long-distance hiking route which, although in some places a little distant from the high 'Berg, makes a fine walk either in its entirety or in stages. Conventionally hikers take five days to make the 60km journey from the start in the Sani Pass to the finish at Bushman's Nek and make overnight stops at the strategically sited KZNW huts, Pholela, Mzimkhulwana, Winterhoek and Swiman, finishing at Bushman's Nek. You may start this hiking tour only at an official starting point and may stay only in overnight facilities provided for this purpose. Tents are not permitted. The cost of the overnight hut stays is subject to change and places must be reserved beforehand. Enquiries and bookings can be made by telephone or letter to: **Reservations Officer**, KwaZulu-Natal Nature Conservation Service, PO Box 13069, Cascades, 3202, tel (033) 845 1000, email: bookings@kznwildlife.com.

What's in a name?

Several legislative procedures have dictated the sometimes confusing designative nomenclature of the various areas which together comprise the Maloti-Drakensberg Park. For the majority of visitors the history and rationale for this is of no immediate interest.

So for clarity, and with no disrespect to some contemporary names, many of which are of Zulu origin, this guide uses names concordant with those on the current relevant maps and those that appear on the official signage at the Park entrances. This applies also to the names of rivers, mountains and places although they may be spelt in different ways in different maps or books, particularly with the recent gradual transition to traditional Zulu names. Visitors will hear Zulu, Afrikaans and English spoken, but English is the language of the tourist industry.

PRE-WALK CHECKLIST

- Plan the day, including a time estimate. Take local advice if available

- Know the route intimately. Assess possible escape routes on the map in case of inclement weather, illness, fatigue etc

- Tell someone precisely your intended route (and stick to it) and what time you expect to return. Complete a walker's register if there is one.

- Ascertain whether any planned vegetation burns (see under Habitats) are taking place and, if so, where

- Check the weather forecast but be prepared for anything. Be particularly wary of lightning, especially from November to early April. Lightning storms often start after 2pm so start your day early. If you are caught get off ridges and summits as quickly as possible. Generally it is safe to shelter in large caves/overhangs.

- Ask about river levels and consider safety before attempting a crossing

- Have a kit checklist available. Always include warm clothing, waterproof jacket and trousers and a small survival bag. Take a whistle, a torch, map, compass and a mobile phone with an emergency number in the contact section. With luck there will be a signal when you need it.

- Pack a first-aid kit

- Take ample water (about two litres per person) and keep a reserve. (You could take less if there is a reliable and safe watering point along the route.)

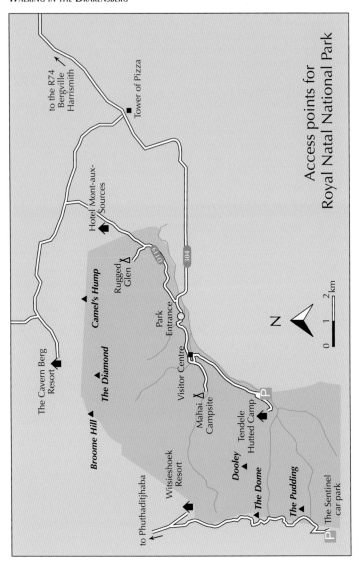

Access points for Royal Natal National Park

to the R74
Bergville
Harrismith

Tower of Pizza

Hotel Mont-aux-Sources

D119

304

Rugged Glen

Park Entrance

Camel's Hump

The Diamond

The Cavern Berg Resort

Broome Hill

to Phuthaditjhaba

Witsieshoek Resort

Visitor Centre

Mahai Campsite

Dooley

Tendele Hutted Camp

The Dome

The Pudding

The Sentinel car park

N

0   1   2 km

ROYAL NATAL NATIONAL PARK (1400M)

Emerging at the top of the Crack (Walk 4)

The Royal Natal National Park (RNNP), isolated from the rest of the original uKhahlamba-Drakensberg Park by the farming area of Mnweni, was so designated in 1916. It attained the additional title of 'Royal' after a visit by the British Royal Family in 1947. It is boomerang-shaped with the short axis facing E and lies with its NW and W sides abutting on the Free State with a southern boundary shared with Lesotho. The principal and world-famous feature is the Amphitheatre, a stunning and sheer basalt wall about 5km in length and over 1000m in height, extending SW from the Sentinel (3165m) to the Eastern Buttress (3045m).

Above the Amphitheatre lies the summit plateau from which a number of domes arise. In 1863 the French missionaries Arbousset and Daumer named the highest of these Mont-aux-Sources (3282m, see Walk 12). This summit lies on the Lesotho border and was so-named as five rivers have their origins in the vicinity. One of these rivers, the famous Thukela (originally Tugela), tumbles down the Amphitheatre in a series of five leaps, together giving a height of 948m. Opinion varies about its position in the world league tables; most give it the accolade of the second highest waterfall in the world after the agreed world champion, the Angel Falls in Venezuela.

The stone navigational and directional markers in this park (prefixed 'R' on the official map) are wonderful examples to others and, presumably, date from a much earlier time. They are generally so good that many visitors eschew the ownership of a map. This is more than just a pity. Maps give us much better orientation, route-finding ability and general information, as well as being indispensable for pre-walk planning. The KZNW map of the area indicates path intersections with the prefix R followed by a number. These are used in the route descriptions below for added clarity.

There are six **start points** for the routes in this section. The visitor centre is well signed as is the car park below the Mahai campsite. The car park below

Thendele Hutted Camp is at the end of the public road that continues from the visitor centre before it rises very steeply. The fourth start point is at the Rugged Glen campsite (or the Mont-aux-Sources Hotel). Walk 12 goes from Sentinel car park, a two-hour drive north of the park entrance and Walk 13 from the Cavern Berg Resort (see directions at the beginning of the route descriptions).

GETTING THERE

From OR Tambo International Airport, Johannesburg

Leave the airport on R24 to join the N3 as described on p35. Follow this for 275km as far as Harrismith. There take slip-road L (No. 29 SP N5 Bethlehem) and continue on N5 for c5km before turning L onto R74 (SP Bergville & Clarens). After another 8km turn L again, staying on R74 (SP Bergville), over Oliviershoek Pass and steeply down its S side. Soon after that multiple signs, including the key one, 'Royal Natal', direct you to turn R on R304 towards the Park that lies some 17km down the road. The visitor centre is 2km down the road after the entrance gate.

From King Shaka International Airport, Durban

Leave the airport via the connection to the N2, the main N–S coastal route. Drive S for about 30km to the interchange with the N3 (SP Pietermaritzburg). Once established on the N3 heading N, take exit 194 and turn L onto R74 (SP Winterton). After going through Winterton and continuing on R74 bypassing Bergville, continue for almost 30km before turning L onto R304 (SP Royal Natal).

FACILITIES

Bergville (47km) has an ATM, post office, pharmacy, supermarket and petrol.

A great feature of the Park is the wide choice of nearby accommodation, probably the best of any area of the Drakensberg. This ranges from bed and breakfast to luxury hotels and 'family resorts'. Particularly recommended is the excellent and family-run Cavern Berg Resort (www.cavern.co.za)

Inside the park the superbly sited and comfortable Thendele Hutted Camp run by KZN Wildlife is self-catering with no restaurant. The Mahai campsite is also beautifully positioned. The Rugged Glen site is rather more basic and outside the park boundary.

Some simple provisions, maps, souvenirs and details of activities including guided walks are available at the visitor centre, but plan on buying all necessary self-catering provisions beforehand. There is no coffee shop or restaurant, a serious oversight in my view offering both revenue and employment opportunities.

MAP REQUIRED

KZN Wildlife uKhahlamba-Drakensberg Park Hiking Map 1

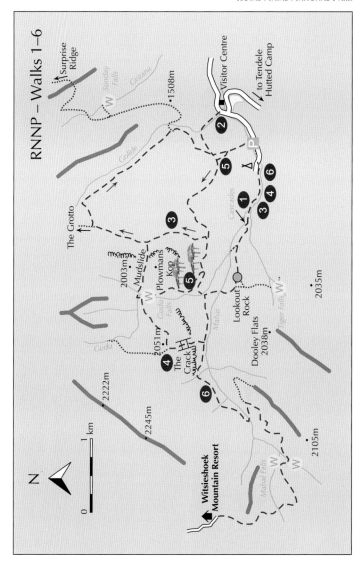

RNNP – Walks 1–6

WALK 1
The Cascades

Start	Car park below the Mahai campsite
Distance	3km
Ascent	Negligible
Grade	Easy
Time	1hr

A great short walk suitable for all. Children aged 0 to 90 will love it.

The Cascades

Leave from the W end of the **car park** on a concrete-slabbed, pushchair-friendly surface with the Mahai stream on the right. Just before the campsite entrance cross the stream on the road bridge and turn left onto the same easy surface. The stream is now on your L. All good things come to an end and this comes to pass just before you re-cross the stream on a hump-backed metal bridge, where the path suddenly becomes decidedly pushchair

unfriendly. After another 200m, just where a large rock seems to impede progress, there is a divergence of ways. Step around the corner on the R and voilà, beautiful **cascades**, small falls of water cut into the underlying sandstone. A great place to while away some time. ▸

Return the same way.

WALK 2

Fairy Glen

Start	Across the road from the visitor centre
Distance	1km
Ascent	Negligible
Grade	Easy
Time	45mins

This is a pleasant little stroll, especially for children, through trees and ending at a waterfall.

The traditional start is on the road into the park almost opposite the visitor centre, indicated by a small sign pointing to a path that dives into a tunnel of woodland. This follows the Golide stream (with the stream on your L) ascending very slightly over rather uneven ground which is unsuitable for pushchairs. After 500m a footbridge takes you over the stream with, on the R, a pool and a very small waterfall. A few metres up the path after the crossing it is possible to turn R and walk across the flat stones that form the top of the waterfall.

Caution here, slippery when wet! We saw a spectacular but inadvertent plunge by a very young lady into the waters below. She swam out and was more concerned about the camera she had been holding – ah, the resilience of the young!

Route-finding difficulties

THE MYSTERY OF FAIRY GLEN

A well-known South African guidebook to the Drakensberg extols the virtues of this walk but relocates it some 2.5km up the Golide valley and quotes 1h each way walking time. We and many others spent some time on that path (which has no forest) searching for the idyllic if elusive glen. Investigation revealed signposts close to the visitor centre and at the Mahai car park to get one going but then …nothing. So where was it? As we stood at path junction R13 talking to an equally puzzled South African family, their 10-year-old daughter pointed out a small concrete square embedded in the earth at our feet which had an arrow pointing us the right way, back towards the visitor centre. So, Angela from Edenvale, thanks again. Mystery solved.

It can be reached also from the Mahai car park via path junction R13 but this is a rather longer walk, but a nice round trip.

This area makes for a good play place shaded by nice deciduous woodland. Behind, a small path leads up R to a more substantial fall, also a nice place to linger. There's nothing sensational about this but it is easy, short, and pleasant for children. Return the same way. ◄

WALK 3
Plowman's Kop Loop

Start	Mahai car park
Distance	10.5km
Ascent	450m
Grade	Moderate
Time	4hrs

A circular tour starting at the car park below the Mahai campsite going W then N before rounding Plowman's Kop and returning via the pretty and tiny Golide valley. The walk up to Lookout Rock is a good, short excursion in its own right.

Start by walking to the **Cascades** (Walk 1). Arriving there go L around the rock following the signpost for 'Tiger Falls' and 'Lookout Rock'. This is a concrete path to reduce erosion and makes for a fast ascent. At c1520m a small unsigned path breaks off R by a stone sign for Lookout Rock. ▶

There are steep sections but they are not persistent and the scenery is distractingly pleasant with small clumps of Protea lining the path. **Lookout Rock** is a mushroom-shaped lump just to the R of the path at c1660m and after 2.5km and 45mins of walking. It lies directly beneath the sandstone buttress of **Dooley Flats**. This excellent viewpoint is the end of a walk for many.

At this point a path joins from the L from Tiger Falls. After the compulsory photo stop, go straight on and almost immediately reach a T-junction. From the L is yet another way from Tiger Falls so turn R and soon descend the steps to cross the **Mahai** stream. On the other side the path climbs gently and continues easily through grassland. After a little more than 3km from the start you arrive at another path junction (R11) which lies just on the edge of woodland and the small Gudu stream. A left turn leads

This leads to McKinley's Pool and goes behind a large boulder to arrive riverside within 100m. It is worth the diversion and a good destination in its own right.

Evening light on Plowman's Kop

up towards Mahai Falls and eventually the Basuto Gate and Witsieshoek Mountain Resort about 6km and 500m climb away (see Walk 6).

Turn R, cross the stream and go into the Gudu Bush, at this point a rather gloomy wooded area although it is airier and brighter higher up. There is some height loss before breaking out of the trees but this has levelled out before you reach a signpost at junction R12. If the day is too hot, the legs too tired or the thirst too pressing there is a short-cut back down to the Mahai car park by turning R and descending the slope, reversing the start of Walk 5.

The signpost here also indicates that a path leads to the 'Hotel'. This refers to the old **Natal National Park Hotel** which has steadily fallen into disrepair since it was last operational in the 1940s. It is adjacent to the Mahai car park.

Now go uphill, signposted to 'The Mudslide', and more or less contour around **Plowman's Kop**, the large mass of hill in front of you. After a short section of rocky steps through woodland you reach an important landmark, the path up to the Mudslide (junction R22). This is the famous or indeed infamous route down from the top of the Little Berg on Plowman's Kop at a point close to **Gudu Falls** (see Walk 4). The route is now restored and open. You can see the bottom of the slide just L of the base of the detached pinnacle. ▶

Go straight on across easy and fairly level ground passing some tree ferns and, after a muddy patch of bushes, zig-zag L and R to a path junction (R23). To continue in the same line would take you up to the Grotto.

The Grotto is a cave-like structure adjoining two small ravines wherein you can clamber, a little more than 1km from path junction R23 referred to above. It is an easy walk. When asked, most people's opinion was that it wasn't worth the effort.

From junction R23 start downhill R. Across the grassland is the **Golide** stream and from there it is a delightful descent, trees huddled over the watercourse with spa pools aplenty but they may be difficult to get to. On the L pass the turn off for Sunday Falls (Walk 10) before winding down to the by now familiar junction R13. Straight on here, pass another junction unmarked on the map, and come down towards the campsite. There is access to it by going R at the fork but keeping L leads down to the car park where you started.

Close by this point a troop of baboons have a popular haunt: even if you don't see them you may well hear them barking noisily.

WALK 4
The Crack and the Mudslide

Start	Mahai car park
Distance	10km to top of Crack and return by same route or via Mudslide
Ascent	550m (750m returning via Mudslide)
Grade	Moderate (L) for the Crack and strenuous (L) for the Mudslide
Time	5hrs (allow 5–6hrs+ if returning via Mudslide)

An excellent outing to a 'must-see' topographic feature and geological oddity. The route up to the grandeur of the Little Berg involves mild scrambling and a chain ladder at an easy angle. The optional descent via the Mudslide is much more challenging but for aficionados the route has been renovated and is open for business.

Follow Walk 3 (Plowman's Kop Loop) up past **Lookout Rock** and on to junction R11 just by the **Gudu** stream. Turn L and climb easily up the path for almost 900m heading up the **Mahai** valley to a junction (R17) where the Crack is signposted off to the R. The way ahead leads further up the Mahai valley, ultimately to the Basuto Gate and Witsieshoek Resort, but that's for another day (see Walk 6).

Turn R here. Until now there has been an impressive and seemingly unassailable rock wall in front but the name of the route gives the game away. As you get closer a fault line in the cliff becomes apparent. At this point the path becomes ridiculously steep and at one point has steps designed for people with extendable legs. There is nothing difficult here, just hard work. Once the trees are reached and a few boulders surmounted, cast your eyes up R and see the extraordinary 'Crack'.

The fun starts here. Initially it is just a walk using hands for balance, soon passing under an overhang on the L side of **the Crack**. Swinging back to the R side you find a small wooden ladder which in turn leads you back L again right up to the rock wall. You are at about half-height now and this is where you meet the 27-rung **chain ladder**. Steadiness is the watchword but very few find it too challenging (climbing aboard for the descent is more awkward and a fixed video camera here might make for some amusing viewing). After this excitement the rest is straightforward, mild scrambling leading to the top where a small path exits L. ◄ You are now established on the Little Berg and when the path curves easily up and round to the R you begin to see the views. Hereabouts are picnic spots galore but a decision needs to be made about your return route. The same way back or the Mudslide?

The Crack is about 100m high

The chain ladder in the Crack

THE MUDSLIDE OPTION

From the top of The Crack a path cuts up R (NE) over a high point (2051m) and becomes a cairned track leading down to cross the Gudu stream just where it disappears over its waterfall on the W side of Plowman's Kop (see Walk 5). Climb a steep grass slope on the opposite bank and then go downhill to reach the unsigned start of the Mudslide, which descends very steeply down a tree- and boulder-littered ravine. Near the top there is a single chain to descend a steep gully and afterwards multiple ladders to overcome awkward sections.

On a fine day, with care, it's all rather fun but it can be extremely precarious in the wet – vouched for by the author!

Leaving the cleft at the foot of the adventure, walk steeply down to a SP (R22). Turn R and continue for almost 1km to another SP (R12). Here go L and meander down to the final SP (now not co-located with R13 but 200m further S). Keep straight on and, after ignoring a small path R to the campsite, go down and cross the river to reach the car park.

WALK 5
Gudu Bush and Gudu Falls

Start	Mahai car park
Distance	9.5km
Ascent	500m
Grade	Moderate
Time	4hrs

An excellent, not-too-long round-trip expedition encompassing great views, some shady if thick forest and a splendid waterfall. The final path up to the falls is not shown on the KZNW map.

At the E end of the **car park** take the path that crosses the river on a bridge and climbs across open country, soon joined from the L by a small path from the campsite. Fork

Gudu Falls

L at the next junction which is unnumbered and barely visible on the map. Soon you are joined from the R by the path from the visitor centre via Fairy Glen. The route climbs easily at first, later steepening only a little to arrive at junction R12 close to the SE corner of the wooded area called the **Gudu Bush**.

Turn L and soon enter the forest where you gain a little more height. Early on a spring morning the place is alive with birdsong. It is necessary to keep a very careful watch for your next turn off, which is on the R and unmarked on the map. The only indication on the ground is a broken stone signpost on the ground. Higher up, don't be alarmed when the path leaves the river on occasion. After more distance and climb than might be expected (about 200m height gain from the main path), you arrive at **Gudu Falls**. ▶

It is unlikely that you will share this destination with others. You can walk behind the curtain of water but beware, it is very slippery back there and an extremely chilly early bath awaits the unwary.

Gloomy it might be on occasion but it is undeniably a superb waterfall and very atmospheric.

61

To make an interesting round trip retrace your steps, and on meeting the main path turn R and continue to the Gudu stream crossing. There is a short cut to the crossing if you can find it on the way down. On the other side of the stream you reach signpost R11, and after taking the L fork simply reverse Walk 3 over **Lookout Rock**, down the steep concrete path, past the **Cascades** and the campsite to the car park.

WALK 6
Witsieshoek via Mahai Falls

Start	Mahai car park
Distance	9km
Ascent	850m
Grade	Moderate
Time	5hrs 30mins

A straightforward and pleasant walk on a good path with good signposting. Interestingly, it doesn't take much longer than driving round to Wisieshoek, but you can't carry a suitcase and you don't have a car at the top for Walk 12. You can hire a guide at Witsieshoek for the ascent to the escarpment plateau (prior booking necessary).

Use directions for Walk 4 until the SP (R17) for the Crack. At this point continue W up the **Mahai valley** with the stream down below to your L. The path is good and the gradient here very gentle. After crossing a stream in a re-entrant the path curves SW and winds up to a small patch of forest with cliffs and a cave to your R. Here it crosses the baby Mahai stream. After another 500m or so you arrive at a SP (R18) where you turn R. (L is for Dooley Flats, a long and ultimately trackless ascent)

It is a bit steeper from here but still easy, up to a series of small **waterfalls** that some maps (but not the official one) call Dooley Water. It is a nice place for a drink. **Mahai Falls** can be seen on the approach to this point above the confluence of Dooley Water and the Mahai itself. From here the route remains straightforward, turning S then resolutely N up to the Basuto Gate and **Witsieshoek**. Note that the steep zig-zags up to the L towards The Nek are now severely eroded and are closed for use.

WALK 7
Thukela Gorge Walk

Start	Car park below Thendele Hutted Camp, just before the R-hand hairpin bend leading up to the camp
Distance	13km to the picnic spot and back
Ascent	400m
Grade	Easy to picnic spot, strenuous subsequently (**L, E**)
Time	5hrs

An extremely popular walk which can be over-busy at weekends, especially at times of public holidays. This is the way to see the Amphitheatre at its absolute best. The views are superb and situations in and around the gorge can be exciting.

Although parking is free there is a local official manning the mountain register which should be completed before setting out and signed again on return. It is customary to give a small gratuity of the order of a few Rand at that time, having first checked that the car is intact.

A signpost for 'Gorge' and other destinations leads to a narrow and often muddy path which meanders SW through shrubs and trees just above the **Thukela** on its N bank. The path continues in the same line for a short

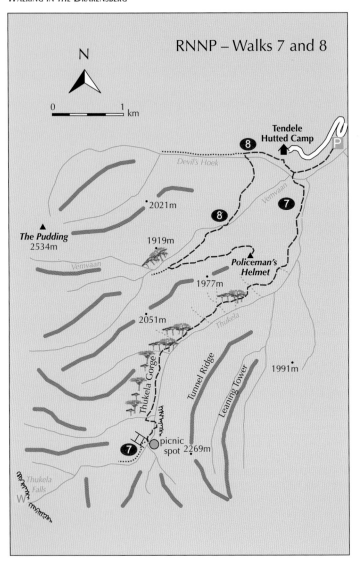

distance along the **Vemvaan** stream after the Thukela, of which the Vemvaan is a tributary, has turned S. After 800m a sign directs you down L to cross the stream on a footbridge, then the easy and obvious path climbs gently back into the Thukela valley through knee-high grassland and many small Protea trees.

For the next 2km or so the path undulates only a little and remains well above the river, gradually veering SW from S, always with the vastly impressive wall of the Amphitheatre ahead. It is always easy to follow and there are no unsigned alternatives to undermine confidence. Occasionally there is a diversion away from the river to cross a subsidiary stream, and later stretches pass through small patches of woodland, blessedly cool on hot days. The path is a bit up and down but always subtly gaining height. As you enter the **Thukela Gorge** proper, with steep rock walls on the R and towering sandstone cliffs opposite, a short descent brings you to the riverside. Cross the river at the easiest spot, walk upstream on the other side and, after

Walking towards the Amphitheatre, en route for Thukela Falls

65

The Thukela at the tunnel-like gorge

about 100m, re-cross. Where to do this is easy to locate. Another 300m and you arrive at 'the picnic spot' – a large and comfortable boulder area at the confluence of the Thukela and the stream running down from Devil's Tooth Gully high up on the L. Most people quit here at the picnic spot and return the same way, but excitement rewards the adventurous. You can either continue through the gorge or by-pass the gorge by a chain ladder for a view of Thukela Falls. Both extensions are outlined below.

Through the gorge: Ahead the Thukela enters what appears to be a tunnel but which in reality is a gorge, albeit decidedly narrow at the top. At normal water levels it is possible to walk most of the way through, but you will get wet feet. The final push through to come out the other side is tricky. Usually the water is sufficiently deep there to make for an awkward exit onto the rocks, but in times of higher water this way is not just dangerous but a potential death trap, so think very carefully before committing to anything therein.

To avoid the gorge: Ignore the white arrow on the rock and instead look R to the 15m-high **chain ladder**. (At the time of our first visit it was in poor repair but scaleable with confidence, wariness and a sprinkling of agility; however, by the time of our visit in 2016 the ladder had been improved.) Having surmounted this a path leads L and to the foot of a near vertical gully in a corner, which you swarm up using a fixed wire, pitons in the rock, tree roots, hands, teeth and adrenaline. From the top the path winds down through thick vegetation back to the Thukela where you can peer into the tunnel from the opposite side. Upstream, boulder-hopping and paddling, you can go as far as you wish or have time for. The farther you go the better the view of the **Thukela Falls**, the more impressive the basalt cliffs and the more enjoyable the experience. ▶

The falls cascade down 947m in five drops and after significant rain are really impressive, but in these conditions the approach is much more difficult.

WALK 8
Policeman's Helmet

Start	Car park below Thendele Hutted Camp
Distance	13km
Ascent	475m
Grade	Moderate
Time	4hrs 30mins

A great walk to a prominent top which looks amazingly like its name. There is an easy scramble to finish. Return the same way.

Follow directions for Walk 7 up to the bridge over the **Vemvaan** stream. At the signpost which indicates Policeman's Helmet go straight on. The narrow concrete-surfaced path turns non-intuitively up and back to the R but soon commonsense prevails and it turns back W at another signpost where the second of the shortcuts to the tented camp leaves R. You are now following the common route to both the Vemvaan and Devil's Hoek valleys. At this point the Vemvaan stream has turned away SW and it is the **Devil's Hoek** stream that you are now following. The path wanders pleasantly along on the level, often at some distance above the river, to the next signpost (R4A). Turn L and go down to cross the stream at a tree-shaded **ford**, the path then climbing easily over a broad shoulder. ◀

There are no prizes for identifying the Policeman's Helmet from here, indeed you can identify the nose and the moustache as well.

The gradient is still easy but by the time you reach the next **ford** (over the Vemvaan) another 100m has been added to the day's total.

From the stream you climb steeply at first, but the angle eases as you head up towards the end of the valley. The map is inaccurate here. The fork that you are seeking (R7) is much further up the valley than the map portrays and the topographic clue is on the R; the large, rounded

sandstone buttress with forest below at the point where the valley becomes much narrower. The stone signpost directs you back almost 180°. The summit of **Policeman's Helmet** is only 60m higher than the signpost but, such is the undulating nature of the way ahead, the actual height gain is much greater. Thirty minutes walking will do it and it is necessary to walk below and past the top before turning back and scrambling up a narrow and slightly exposed ramp to the excellent summit. ▶

Policeman's Helmet

There aren't many luncheon stops with better views and ambience.

WALK 9
Camel's Hump

Start	Rugged Glen campsite car park or the Hotel Mont-aux-Sources
Distance	10km there and back: 15km returning via Sunday Falls
Ascent	500m there and back: 650m returning via Sunday Falls
Grade	Moderate
Time	4hrs there and back: 5hrs returning via Sunday Falls

Most walkers enjoy reaching a top. This is another good one, a bit off the beaten track and not achieved without a bit of hard work. You don't meet many other souls up there. There are several options for your return journey.

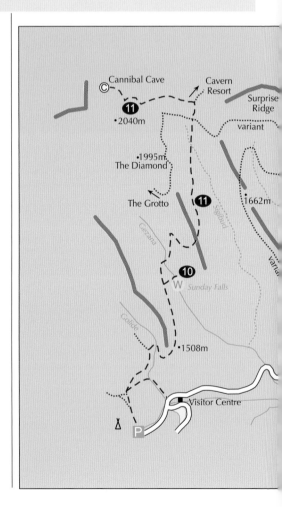

From the Rugged Glen campsite car park, walk to the sign saying 'Ranger's Residence – private no entry'. Ignore this warning and continue up the road for just 15m where on the R you will find a very small path. Blink and you'll miss it. It runs parallel to the W side of

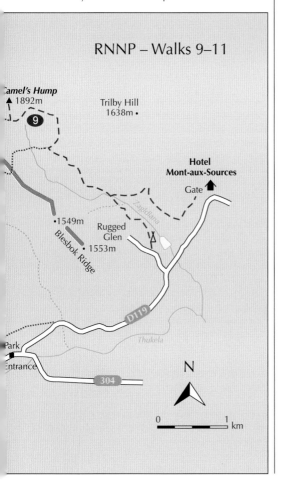

RNNP – Walks 9–11

Camel's Hump
▲ 1892m

9

Trilby Hill
1638m •

**Hotel
Mont-aux-Sources**

Gate ⬆

Zigialana

•1549m

Rugged
Glen

Blesbok Ridge

• 1553m

D119

Thukela

Park

Entrance

304

N

0   1 km

the campsite wood to cross grassland, a tributary and then the main valley stream, the **Zagldlana**. A short distance uphill from the stream and you join alternative (b) at junction R34, c1425m.

From Hotel Mont-aux-Sources, leave through the gate in the fence opposite timeshare villa 18. When visited in 2008 this path was very overgrown but essentially traversed a balcony of grass, ferns and patches of forest. After crossing three respectable streams the path joins that of option (a) at a signpost (junction R34).

After crossing another stream the path steepens and climbs through grassland to a scenic plateau. Camel's Hump is directly in front at this stage, the rocky knoll on the R with the rounded grassy highest point on the L. Keep on in the same line towards the mountain until you meet another path running W–E across your front and turn R (E) here.

Further along this path runs below a large tree-filled basin, thus approaching Camel's Hump from the SE. The perimeter fence of the park looms in front of you at c1700m and you take a sharp L-hand bend at that point, passing just above the basin referred to earlier.

In autumn 2008 there was no sign of a path from here to the summit. The path that you are on contours nicely at c1770m and so, somewhere along here due S of the top, it is easy to take a direct line. After 15mins of long grass, small Proteas and sandstone outcrops the top of **Camel's Hump** will be yours. It is very easy and well worth the effort, as the view all around is magnificent. There is a narrow rocky track leaving the summit W but this ends up on the 'wrong' side of a barbed wire fence so technically is outside the park on private land. However, it is an easier way down so if a walker has inadvertently strayed this way he or she can locate the upper end of the fence and climb easy rocks at that point to get over, limiting the trespass.

The question now arises, which route back? There are **three decent possibilities**.

Camel's Hump

The **first** is simply to reverse your ascent route which will take something under 2hrs. The main advantage of this is that transport is not required. A **second** choice is to reverse the route as far as the last path junction and then continue W to eventually run S along the ridge above the Sigibud valley. This leaves 2km of road walk back up to Rugged Glen. The **final option** makes for a nicer, albeit much longer, walk. Continue W along the contour path as far as the signpost just below **Surprise Ridge** at junction R25. By turning S it is easy to reverse Walk 11, past **Sunday Falls** and through **Fairy Glen** to hit the road at the **visitor centre**. This will take up to 3hrs from Camel's Hump but it is important to consider how you would return to the start point if your transport is stranded there. It is a long haul back up and there are no taxis.

WALK 10
Sunday Falls

Start	Visitor centre or Mahai car park
Distance	7km
Ascent	150m
Grade	Easy
Time	2hrs 30mins

A highly recommended walk on good paths without any navigational difficulty, leading to a nice picnic spot with a stream and a waterfall.

There are two options for the first section of this walk.

From the visitor centre: Follow directions for Walk 2 to Fairy Glen. After passing Fairy Glen the path curves W to reach a very familiar path intersection (R13) and signpost. Anyone walking in this area for any length of time will soon become familiar with this signpost and this is the intersection with the second option.

From Mahai car park: At the E end of the car park take the path that crosses the river on a bridge and climbs across open country, soon joined L by a small path from the campsite, and fork R at the junction only faintly seen on the map, soon reaching junction R13.

The now common route heads off NE and goes easily up to the point where the path divides (junction R29). Here turn R as signed and immediately cross the **Golide** stream. Surmount the easy shoulder into the **Gezana valley**, turning gradually N and, having travelled about 1.3km from the Golide stream crossing, reach another path junction (R27) with a directional sign R for **Sunday Falls**. It is plain sailing from here. Go gently downhill for some 300m to a great flat, smooth slab of rock over which the river flows

shallowly just before it plunges down the large falls to your R. It is a good place to stop.

To see the falls properly find the little path on the opposite bank which winds downhill through the trees to the foot of the cascade. Return the same way. ▶

The only disturbance here is likely to be from a noisy troop of baboons, but on our return journey we surprised a Black-backed Jackal doing a daylight territorial reconnaissance.

The path to Sunday Falls, leading down to the head of the gorge

At 22m height it is no wonder of the world, but it is a good place to end a walk.

WALK 11
Surprise Ridge and Cannibal Cave

Start	Visitor centre or Mahai car park
Distance	19km
Ascent	500m
Grade	Moderate
Time	6hrs

A moderately long but easy out-and-back through grassland with an historic cave to round off the proceedings.

This section of the walk is both easy and peaceful. You look over rolling grassland dotted with ferns and Protea trees.

Start as for Sunday Falls (Walk 10). Instead of turning R to access the falls at path junction R27 go straight on and cross the **Gezana** upstream from the falls at c1550m. The interest continues with a zig-zag height-gaining routine up the hillside to eventually round a **shoulder** and ease down into the valley of the **Sigibud** stream. ◄ There is a small descent to cross a stream into a small wooded area and then the path continues with the stream on the L. The small gorge ahead is lovely and you pass through the base of it before climbing out R. The map reflects none of this, presumably because of scale.

After resuming a northerly course go over a small brow and see the shallow pass ahead which is where you meet **Surprise Ridge**. Just a few minutes before this there is a crossroads (junction R25): to the R (E) lies Camel's Hump, to the L (W) the long path eventually leading round The Diamond and Castle Rock to the Grotto. But today's route lies straight ahead, through the gate which marks the boundary of the RNNP and onto private land with its permissive path. You reach the crest of the ridge at a crossroads c1830m with about 7km on the clock. Ahead and below you can see The Cavern Resort Hotel (see note at end of this section).

Cannibal Cave and Cold Ridge from Surprise Ridge

Turn L and follow the path which takes a direct line towards **Cannibal Cave**, 1.5km away. It is easy to follow and after a gentle downhill section it veers R towards a wooded re-entrant. Keep L when you meet the ascent path from The Cavern Hotel and after the trees you arrive at the large cave.

CANNIBAL CAVE

Cannibal Cave

The Zulu King Shaka, who began his rule around 1818, despatched forces to plunder and conquer other tribes. Many of those potential victims fled into the Drakensberg, some finding shelter in the overhang known now as Cannibal Cave. The name tells its own story of the privations they suffered and their sometime solution to starvation. It is not known how long they remained there.

WALK 12

Top of Thukela Falls and
Mont-aux-Sources (3282m)

Start	Sentinel car park above Witsieshoek
Distance	10km to the top of Thukela Falls: 16km to Mont-aux-Sources summit
Ascent	500m via the ladders: 600m via Kloof Gully. If descending via the gully add 150m of climb. To summit of Mont-aux-Sources 800m
Grade	Moderate via Kloof Gulley, strenuous (E and L) via the chain ladders
Time	5hrs or 6hrs to the summit

A straightforward walk to the escarpment plateau and including optionally an ascent of the famous chain ladders. The disadvantage is the somewhat long and awkward access by road (but see Walk 6).

In early 2016 there were incidents of Basotho people aggressively demanding money or food at the top of the chain ladders. The current local recommendation is to do this walk accompanied by a guide that will, in any case, enhance the experience. Work is in hand to remedy the situation but, even if resolved, it would be wise to seek local advice before you set off.

GETTING TO THE SENTINEL CAR PARK

From the RNNP, go back to R74 and turn L onto it. Cross Oliviershoek Pass and continue to the T-junction with R712. Turn L and go along R712 as far as the crossroads with R57 where you turn L (SP Phuthaditjhaba). From this long, rather straggling town, the Witsieshoek Mountain Resort is well-signposted. It takes you through Phuthaditjhaba on a well-surfaced undulating road some 15km to a fork. To the left is the Resort Hotel, to the right the very rough road to the Sentinel car park, negotiable by normal cars if you keep a strict lookout for large stones and potholes. The journey takes about 2 hours (about 100km). You can stay at the Resort Hotel which is community-owned (tel 0027 58 713 6361).

The path round the Sentinel from near the chain ladders. Kloof Gully is on the right

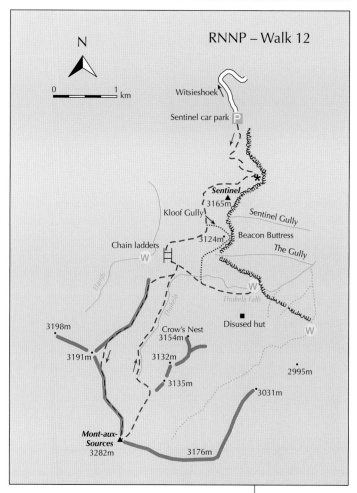

The path starts there and, after a level section, zig-zags its way up below the Sentinel, its bulky rectangular mass forming both the northern boundary of the Drakensberg and the right-hand end of the Amphitheatre when

Climbers on the chain ladders

seen from the usual angle. A SP offers you the choice of proceeding directly on your way or going L to the viewpoint. Visit the **viewpoint**. The whole of the Amphitheatre wall right round to Devil's Tooth and the

Eastern Buttress is laid out before you, and the diversion adds very little distance.

The path, exposed in places but not too narrow, winds round behind **the Sentinel** and, at the point where it makes its last dramatic turn R (SW) on the journey to the chain ladders (3.6km from the CP at c2905m), **Kloof Gully** rises steeply to your L and up to **Beacon Buttress**. This is an excellent alternative to taking on the ladders for the ascent to the plateau and it rises about 230m emerging at c3140m. In descent this gully has a stonefall problem to be aware of and is hard on tired legs, but for those who decline the chain-ladder experience it is a good way up. From the top of the gully a good path descends to the **Thukela** stream and joins the path from the top of the ladders.

> **The ladder option:** For ladder afficionados the path continues as a traverse for c1km before turning up into a rocky bay. This route dates from 1930. There are two **ladders** parallel to each other rising vertically about 17m up the rock wall at which point you dismount and climb aboard one of the next pair, much shorter at about 13m. They are well maintained and relatively stable. After a short walk at the top of the second ladder you emerge at a large cairn on the plateau. A good path leads down to the **Thukela** stream. The path now leads onward to the very lip of the famous **Thukela Falls**. It is worth remembering that in spring, especially September before the the rainy season, the falls may be completely dry.

For Mont-aux-Sources use the ladders to save time and effort. After descending the path for a few metres veer R and get onto the obvious **ridge** running SW, taking in **pt3191m** before turning S to gain the rocky summit of **Mont-aux-Sources**. In descent it is easiest to walk down NNE to pick up the infant **Thukela** and follow its L bank back down until you can intersect the path back to the ladders. It is a historical, topographical journey more than 'ooh-aah' territory.

THE CAVERN BERG RESORT

This hotel has been run by the Carte family since 1941 and lies just outside the RNNP over its northern boundary, easily accessible from R74 by taking the usual road towards the RNNP and turning R (signposted) after c8km, just after the 'Tower of Pizza'. It is 10km up there at the very end of the road. It is a fine place to stay and its grounds provide excellent birdwatching and are extensive enough to allow long walks. Indeed, it makes for high-quality hard walking with extremely good guides. As it is outside the RNNP and the uKhahlamba - Drakensberg Park it is beyond the scope of this book but perhaps just one route as a taster is permissible.

There are walking paths direct to the top of Gudu Falls via Plowman's Kop (see related Walk 4) and direct to Witsieshoek (see Walk 13 for reference). Neither of these paths is marked on the KZNW map. Also it is easy to access the RNNP perfectly legitimately over the saddle on Surprise Ridge (see Walk 11).

WALK 13
The Sugar Loaf (2085m)

Start	Cavern Berg Resort
Distance	7km
Ascent	600m
Grade	Moderate
Time	3hrs 30mins

An easy walk to a good summit with interest maintained all the way. Antelope are often seen hereabouts and we encountered Eland, Mountain Reedbuck, Grey Rhebok and Common Duiker as well as a Black-backed Jackal. The Sugar Loaf is not named on the KZNW map.

Leave the hotel up the surfaced road for a few metres to a gate. Follow the red arrow up the track R. Pass the soccer field and take the L fork, following another red arrow. Go straight up to a gap in the fence where a small reservoir,

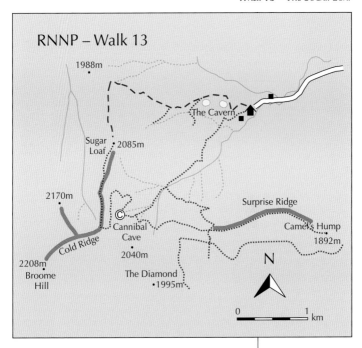

RNNP – Walk 13

1988m

The Cavern

Sugar
Loaf • 2085m

2170m

© Cannibal
Cave

Surprise Ridge

Cold Ridge

Camel's Hump
1892m

2208m
Broome
Hill

The Diamond
•1995m

2040m

N

0   1
km

Wattle Dam, is close to you on the L. The path divides
again here – L is for Surprise Ridge, but you go straight on
(SP for Sugar Loaf). Further on is another gate after which
there is a short steep section taking you onto a small plateau. Another fork indicates Lone Rock to the L but go R
and steeply up again. Ahead you will see the cleft in the
rocks that is Sugar Loaf Gap. Don't be distracted by a
path going R along the base of the rocks.

The way up to Sugar Loaf Gap is steep and rocky
but presents no difficulty. At the Gap turn L and in a few
metres you will see the upland plateau with flat sandstone outcrops and, ahead, the appropriately-named
Sugar Loaf. A path leads directly towards it and the final
few metres are very steep but easy. ▶

Retrace your steps to descend.

Just before the
top look out for
the interesting
iron oxide uplifts
in the sandstone,
looking uncannily
like the remnants
of fence posts.

The Sugar Loaf

Local guides have other interesting alternatives on offer from this point, including a descent via Cavern Gap (steep and rough) to **Cannibal Cave** (see Walk 11) and thence directly back to the Hotel.

Note that the path S from the summit goes up to Cold Hill (c2187m) and, after a col, contours around the base of **Broome Hill** (2208m) which can be climbed easily in a few minutes. The path itself offers access to the top of Gudu Falls and a direct route to Witsieshoek.

CATHEDRAL PEAK (1480M)

Looking back towards Cathedral Peak on the way to Tryme Hill

Even before you drive in through the Park entrance and on towards the Cathedral Peak Hotel it hits you. These are serious and high mountains, much more in your face than in the Royal Natal. This is a world of massive rock buttresses, towering crags and pinnacles, deep clefts and valleys between. At this point the main Drakensberg ridge runs roughly NW–SE with a subsidiary ridge breaking off at about 90°. This line of peaks points NE starting with Mitre (3023m) and, after the Inner Horn (3005m), Outer Horn (3005m) and the eponymous Bell (2928m), ends with Cathedral Peak itself (3004m). Why Cathedral Peak is so-named remains something of a mystery for it bears no resemblance whatsoever to a Cathedral. A long time ago, probably before 1905, it had been called Zikhali's Horn after a local chief. It has been suggested that a transposition of names took place with a peak now called the Rockeries some 11km away. An old map names this latter peak 'The Cathedral'.

On the main escarpment ridge itself there is a bunch of even bigger summits, pride of place going to Cleft Peak (3281m). Add the large areas of Little Berg grassland to this and it is immediately clear that there is a lot to see and explore. All walks in this section start from the Cathedral Peak Hotel complex.

GETTING THERE

From OR Tambo International Airport, Johannesburg
Follow the N3 (SP Durban) to exit 230, turning E on N11 towards Ladysmith. After about 6km turn R onto R600 (SP Winterton) and continue back over the N3 to reach Winterton itself. The R600 leads round the E side of the town and goes R at the traffic lights. After crossing the river turn R for Cathedral Peak, 38km away.

From King Shaka International Airport, Durban
Leave the airport via the connection to the N2, the main N–S coastal route. Drive S for about 30km to the interchange with the N3 (SP Pietermaritzburg). Once established on the N3 heading N take exit 194 and turn L onto R74 (SP Winterton), after 25km going through Winterton and turning L at the traffic lights onto R600 as above.

FACILITIES

Winterton has an ATM, Post Office, pharmacy, supermarket and petrol.

There is no accommodation outside the Park within easy distance.

Inside the Park there is a campsite and the KZN Wildlife hutted camp at Didima with its attractive self-catering chalets, a small shop with basic provisions and a restaurant. This complex is co-located with the Didima San Art Centre, well worth a visit. Here there is also the possibility of a guided tour to a rock art site. A little further into the Park lies the famous and very comfortable Cathedral Peak Hotel (www.cathedralpeak.co.za) which well-deserves its excellent reputation.

Walkers who are not staying at the hotel and not intending to visit the bar should use the visitor car park on the L side of the access road opposite the golf course.

MAP REQUIRED

KZN Wildlife uKhahlamba-Drakensberg Park Hiking Map 2

WALK 14
Doreen Falls

Start	The sundial in Cathedral Peak Hotel
Distance	4km
Ascent	75m
Grade	Easy
Time	1hr 30mins

A much-favoured and easy, short out-and-back to a pleasant little waterfall. Almost everyone can do it.

Doreen Falls

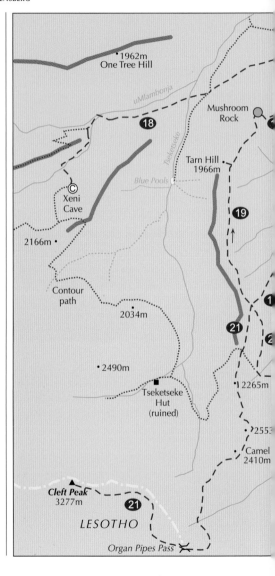

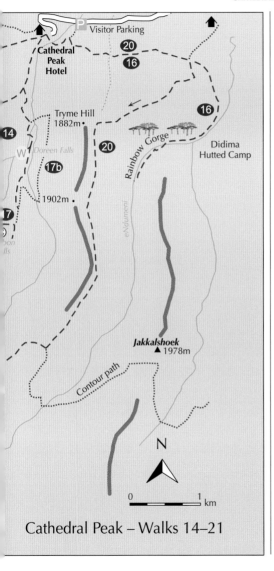

Visitor Parking

Cathedral
Peak
Hotel

20
16

Tryme Hill
1882m

14

16

W Doreen Falls

Rainbow Gorge

Didima
Hutted Camp

17b

20

eNdumeni

1902m

7

bon
lls

Jakkalshoek
▲ 1978m

Contour path

N

0   1 km

Cathedral Peak – Walks 14–21

Head out of the hotel through the accommodation by the signposted route and go along the road to the cell-phone mast. Just after this a sign directs you down diagonally L keeping the extensive stables area to the R. Ignore a small path forking L and go straight ahead at a crossroads. After about 1km the path forks. Go L (R fork is for Mushroom Rock). Next cross a **stream** and go up stony steps on the other bank, curving round to the R to arrive at a junction by the first of two old stone signs. Go straight ahead, up more steps and onto level ground where there is another fork and a second ancient stone sign just before it on the L. So far it is about 2km from the hotel. The R fork here re-crosses the stream and leads to **Doreen Falls** within about 200m: the L fork is for Ribbon Falls (Walk 17).

WALK 15
Mushroom Rock

Start	The sundial in Cathedral Peak Hotel
Distance	5km
Ascent	400m
Grade	Easy
Time	3hrs

A fairly short walk to a visually striking geological feature. However, there is a tough and steep final section, but it is without any technical difficulty or exposure.

There is good scenery all around.

Start as for Doreen Falls (Walk 14) and follow this for 1.2km to the **fork** with a signpost directing you R. Height gain starts immediately and soon you will see the small dam on the R. There is a flat middle section but soon you climb up steeply again using a small wooden ladder in one place. ◀ The last bit is steeply stepped and this

At Mushroom Rock

makes for a strenuous last 50m of height gain. You can go through the hole in the mushroom easily and pose appropriately for a photo. If you continue higher, in the direction of Tarn Hill, be careful; it is quite narrow just above with a big drop on the W and N sides of the ridge. Return the same way.

WALK 16
Rainbow Gorge

Start	Cathedral Peak Hotel Reception
Distance	15km
Ascent	350m
Grade	Moderate in its entirety (T) : easy if you just go a little way upstream
Time	6hrs

For some, this walk offers a strenuous adventure through forest, over rock and into water: for others it could be just a gentle walk to a pleasant stream with nice places to stop. In its entirety it is quite exceptional. **Assess very carefully the depth and current before committing.**

Leave the Hotel Reception heading uphill, and after 100m go down L at a signpost, past the vegetable garden and across the **stream**. Just on the other bank is another sign-post which directs you towards your destination. Just 700m further on turn R at the fork, again signposted (the L fork goes down to the visitor car park about 500m away). The way is pleasant and easy as it crosses rolling grassland on a good path gaining little height.

Soon you arrive above Didima Camp from where a concrete path joins L. This is a **signposted crossroads.** The Tryme Hill path leaves up to the R but your way is straight on. Gradually turn Tryme Hill and the path veers S and descends. There is an excellent view of a sandstone but-tress topped by the grass of the Little Berg with the escarp-ment as a backdrop, all sitting neatly in the **confluence** of the valley streams ahead. The R-hand valley is where Rainbow Gorge lies and the path now descends moder-ately steeply to enter the riverine forest. ◀ The stream on the L becomes increasingly noisier as you get ever nearer the valley floor. Once there the path undulates just above the stream. Anywhere along this section is a good place for those undertaking the short version of the outing to call a halt.

Magical is a reasonable word to use here. It is shady and cool with shafts of sunlight beaming through the trees at unexpected moments as you turn each corner.

Subsequently there are places where investigative prowess is required to tease out the correct way but this is never irremediable. By now you've walked about 5.5km and it is time to play the game 'crossing the river'. It is blindingly obvious that after significant rain the water will be deeper, the crossings more difficult, your feet wet-ter. Indeed, you may judge it hazardous to cross at all. That's your decision. Sometimes the path on the oppo-site bank is less than clear but persistence pays off. We crossed seven times on the way upstream and five times

The chockstone in Rainbow Gorge

on the return, the difference being explained by the discovery of a cunningly concealed tiny path on a rocky ledge unseen in ascent.

At one point there seems to be an impasse when boulders block the route but the R-hand side is easily climbable. Then you reach Rainbow Gorge proper. It is very narrow and, although you can sometimes sneak upstream pressed close to one of the towering side walls precariously balanced on the only dry pebble in sight to remain mostly dry shod, generally it is easier to march resolutely if squelchily up the middle. Here you see the renowned chockstone, jammed between the high walls of the by now very narrow and dark gorge. It looks low and small when first seen from a distance, but as you get closer, water dripping from above, it looks more impressive. Standing underneath defines the formal end of the journey but adventurous souls explore further. Return the same way. ◀

We didn't see rainbows or other spectral phenomena on our visit but it is a superlative gorge walk.

WALKS 17 AND 17B
Ribbon Falls

Start	The sundial in Cathedral Peak Hotel
Distance	7km
Ascent	350m
Grade	Easy
Time	3hrs

A walk with mild scrambling into a small amphitheatre and a nice waterfall to finish, especially splendid after decent rainfall. Hardy folk can walk through the fall and pose for an heroic photograph behind the curtain. There is also easier version of the route outlined below.

This starts along the route of the Doreen Falls walk (Walk 14): indeed you get within 200m of the falls to the point just after the second old stone 'Doreen Falls' signpost, where there is an unsigned L fork. Take this. From here this path is not marked on the KZNW map.

Immediately the steepness kicks off in the direction of a sandstone buttress. (If the path goes down towards a stream you've turned off too soon – see option b of this route). You start on a low but narrow ridge with the main valley stream on your L and the Ribbon Falls/Doreen Falls stream to your R. A little scramble takes you up to a ladder designed for a giant and at the top a rock wall looms. You're trapped. But no, the path sidles off to the R on a small ledge where care is required, especially in the wet.

At a triangular rock the path turns back 180° and the small amphitheatre looms into view with the first glimpse of the falls. The flat-topped ridge is a rocky pavement here, and from the L comes a small path that is the alternative way up (or down). Just ahead at c1780m the path divides, the L turn heading for the Little Berg and higher things, the straight ahead option for you. Note the **cave** on the L just 400m from the junction before the waterfall.

Ribbon Falls

The Easy option (17b): Use the same Doreen Falls route as the main route but turn L at the first stone sign rather than the second. It looks and is little used and runs downhill to cross the valley **stream**. Up the other side is a path junction at which you turn R. After a period of walking above and parallel to this stream go down and re-cross it back to the **W bank** whereupon it soon turns 180° to climb up through sandstone, emerging on the ridge where you join the main route. This way is easier if just a little longer, and is the route indicated on the KZNW map.

WALK 18

Xeni Cave

Start	The sundial in Cathedral Peak Hotel
Distance	11km
Ascent	550m
Grade	Moderate
Time	6hrs

A walk without technical difficulty, but it requires some navigational confidence and a spirit of adventure. It ends at a typical large cave with a waterfall and great views.

Leave the hotel as for Walk 14, heading along the road by the cell-phone mast. From there keep going up the concrete road towards the helipad, which is signed. Pass to the L of the house and, tucked away behind it, take the path up to the football field, favoured by the raucous Hadeda Ibis who often sit on the crossbar. After crossing the field the path begins its gradual descent towards the Tseketseke stream. You are heading directly towards the uMamblonja valley, the stream of the same name

marrying the Tseketseke and running down NE towards the trout hatchery. Take the **R fork** where the path splits and then, after crossing a small stream, find a triangular direction stone.

Go straight ahead (L is for Blue Pools) and cross the **Tseketseke** stream, then follow the S bank of the **uMlambonja** on an undulating path. In autumn this can be an awkward stretch with hugely tall grass above head height obscuring everything underfoot. After rain it is particularly uncomfortable. Although it is not shown on the map, you cross the stream coming down from the Xeni cave valley just above its confluence with the uMlambonja and then keep between the two streams to a low concrete signpost at just over 4km. Fork L here and follow the obvious path until, after 300m, you meet the **Xeni** stream. Cross and 50m up re-cross to the E bank. ▸ Keep on a faint path on this side of the stream until it disappears and then take to the boulders along the stream itself. Flooding regularly removes paths and cairns hereabouts.

At almost 1km from the SP where you forked left there is a very narrow and deeply cut wooded valley going up

The key to locating the final path to Xeni Cave (C) is this rocky wall with its rivulet and, 40m upstream, the small path (marked with a red arrow above)

At this point note the small cave with sleeping places for an emergency such as rain or thunderstorm.

Inside Xeni Cave

A waterfall from above falling over the roof centrally provides both drinking water and shower facilities.

SE from the stream opposite a large rocky buttress to the R. It has a path and leads to a small cave. This is NOT Xeni cave and is un-named. So continue upstream for a further 300m, keeping as close as possible to the steep ground on your L. There you will find a high rocky wall with a rivulet running down over its surface. This comes from a tiny stream in the deep cleft above. Walk another 40m upstream to where the rocky wall gives way to steep grassland. This is the spot where the Xeni cave path starts (see photograph). It zig-zags up steeply, always on the grass, and ultimately turns back L and round into the small grove of trees that partially hides the large overhang which is **Xeni Cave**. Return the same way. ◄

WALK 19
The Tarn Hill Circuit

Start	The sundial in Cathedral Peak Hotel
Distance	8km
Ascent	650m
Grade	Moderate
Time	4hrs

A superb encounter with the Little Berg. Great views and situations, not too long, not too steep. The walk follows the Ribbon Falls route out (Walk 17), then heads up onto the Little Berg, returning via Tarn Hill.

Start this fine walk by following the Ribbon Falls route (Walk 17) all the way to the **path junction** just before **Ribbon Falls**. Turn L there. A steep rocky path leads up to the grassland of the Little Berg, gloriously desolate with a backdrop of spiky mountains. Below on the R a brook babbles its way downhill over small falls and through pools. It is a peaceful place. Also, it is the hunting ground for Jackal Buzzards so look out for the characteristic orange-ginger triangular tail which is only evident during flight. You are heading roughly SW over easy ground towards the two humped hills called, with some licence, the Camel. About 1.5k from the Ribbon Falls junction and just above the 2000m level an old jeep track crosses your path. This intersection is shown on the map but the leftward extension of the track is not shown – for a more detailed description of the anatomy hereabouts see Walk 20.

Turn R here and gain a little height before the path veers round almost to the E before zig-zagging down N to pass between the cairned top of pt2014m and, on the L, a small unnamed conical hill. This takes you through what feels like a small valley to emerge on the plateau of **Tarn Hill** itself. There is a small tarn as shown on the map but it is seasonally dry. The top of Tarn Hill is marked slightly more substantially than other tops hereabouts with a cairn and a metal post. ▶ It is not much of a top in other respects, more of a pimple on a plateau, but a barely perceptible path on your L makes a visit marginally easier.

Next continue easily down to **Mushroom Rock**. Just before you get there, and just as thoughts turn to the photographic opportunities and the position of the sun, the excitement of a very narrow and exposed section of path presents itself. But it is very short and quickly you can pop down to the R and into the hole of the Mushroom. After passing through the hole the way down to the R is obvious.

The outlook from here makes it, with Tryme Hill, one of the must-visit viewpoints of the area.

Thunderclouds gathering over the mountains from the summit of Tarn Hill

This is very steep with giant steps, awkward for short legs and hard on everyone's knees. When wet it can be very treacherous. It is a bit less than 400m descent to the hotel and signs and commonsense bring you down safely.

WALK 20
Tryme Hill and the Contour Path

Start	Cathedral Peak Hotel Reception
Distance	18km
Ascent	900m
Grade	Moderate
Time	5hrs 30mins

A tough walk in its entirety but worth it for breathtaking views and surroundings, varied terrain and a real chance of antelope sightings.

Follow the route for Walk 16 (Rainbow Gorge) as far as the **crossroads** above Didima Camp and about 45min out from the hotel. Turn R here and head up away from the crossroads for Tryme Hill – this is where the hard work begins. It is seriously steep and if ever there were zig-zags they have long since disappeared. So it is nose to the ground for a fast 200m of ascent up between the buttresses. At the first crest the gradient eases and decent hairpin bends appear after you pass the head of a re-entrant on your L. The next crest gives even more encouragement; the final rise to the top of **Tryme Hill** is in sight. From this angle it appears deceptively conical with the path contouring around on the E, your side.

Walking up to the top, just a few metres cross-country, is highly recommended. Surprisingly it turns out to be a large plateau but the actual **summit** is represented by a sad, small pile of stones far off to the R. Surely such a fine viewpoint should be marked in a more splendid way. The whole range of the Cathedral Peak range is visible from here, with views farther afield too. As you swing round from that summit past the Pyramid and Organ Pipes Pass you finish up at the renowned flat top of Cathkin Peak. It was while we were on Tryme Hill that a Bearded Vulture

Tryme Hill from the south

performed an initial fly-past, followed by several close inspections 15m above our heads, perhaps assuming that we were an unusual type of feeding station.

Leave the top S where there is straightforward access back to the original path, which then continues easily along the undulating S ridge of the mountain. Down to the L the ground falls away into the valley of the eNdumeni and Rainbow Gorge, and the route runs parallel to this for the next 3km or so. Soon the path gains a little height on its southward trek and veers SW to arrive at the T-junction with the Contour Path (c1980m). A faint path, unmarked on the map, goes straight ahead but should be ignored. Turn R (W) and follow the Contour Path, still gaining height slowly, as it curves into a deep re-entrant. This is where things get confusing. The best plan from here is to continue on the obvious old jeep track N and then gradually turn W to arrive at the junction with the path from Ribbon Falls (c2020m). The confusion arises because this route is not marked on the map. The Contour Path continues NW from this point but it is barely discernable.

Now it is decision time. Either turn N and head down past **Ribbon Falls** (following Walk 17, the quickest route) or continue W and return via **Tarn Hill** and **Mushroom Rock** (Walk 19). It will be clear that Walks 17, 19 and 20 are interchangeable in so far as one can use any two of them in any order to achieve a round trip.

WALK 21

Organ Pipes Pass and Cleft Peak

Start	The sundial in Cathedral Peak Hotel
Distance	18km to Organ Pipes Pass (22km to Cleft Peak)
Ascent	1600m (1900m to Cleft Peak)
Grade	Strenuous (E)
Time	8hrs (10hrs to Cleft Peak)

A tough excursion, even tougher if you include Cleft Peak in the same day. The route is mostly on a good path, but with significant exposure in places at the top end of the route. The scenery is grand and it is a good and quick way of getting onto the escarpment from Cathedral Peak Hotel.

Follow the route for Walk 19 to the old jeep road. Go straight on up the grassy slope to intersect with the Contour Path and cross it. From this point onward the KZNW map is inaccurate for quite a way, but there's only one path that could possibly be yours.

Go very steeply up the crest of the knoll in front of you and soon the path sidles down its L (E) side. It remains on the same side of the next knoll and goes into a gap. ▶ Scramble up steeply for a few metres before the path resumes on the L side of yet another knoll (**pt 2553**), soon arriving at the first 'hump' of **the Camel**. The path continues on the L side of this but descends sharply into the gap between the two humps, continuing subsequently on the R (W) side of the second hump.

For those who enjoy occasional exposure the fun starts here.

The Camel and Organ Pipes Pass

Two subsidiary pinnacles are passed also on the R before you veer L and go up steeply to round a shoulder which comes down from the main bulk of the mountain. This takes you to a crossing of a stream bed (often dry), the path next climbing up over steep grassy slopes to a detached rocky pinnacle. Ahead and above lies a very narrow boulder gully between the main mass of the mountain and an isolated spike of rock. Some good old-fashioned scrambling is needed here with no particular difficulty.

Up until now there has been a fair degree of exposure to complement the narrow path, but the final section is easy. Leave the gully and go R and down to join a small

The scramble at the rock pinnacle

path coming up from Arendsig. It lies in a broad grassy valley and the top of **Organ Pipes Pass** is just a short walk up here, marked by a large cairn.

For those whose muscles need further exercise, go R and round a small rocky wall and take a more or less direct line up to the R-hand end of the summit ridge of **Cleft Peak** which looms large to the NW. Walk along the ridge to the easy, rocky summit with its attendant cliff. Well done. All that remains is the walk back along the same route.

WALK 22
Baboon Rock

Start	The Golf Club
Distance	9km
Ascent	550m
Grade	Moderate (E)
Time	4hrs

A relatively short excursion to a well-known local feature with some interesting mountain situations en route. Why the name? Because it looks like one.

Most people walk to the golf club from the hotel, down the road and over the Indiana Jones suspension bridge (author's name) and this distance is included in the statistics above. A 'Lake William' signpost at the club-house directs you N up and across a fairway – avoid the green and listen carefully for shouts of warning or anger. Another signpost indicates R but almost immediately head up L on a mown grass track which climbs steadily into a shallow valley. At the mountain bike signs turn R and go up to the signposts. Fork R. At the crest of the small rise that you are approaching is a stone signpost at a crossroads. Turn L and get established on a ridge which

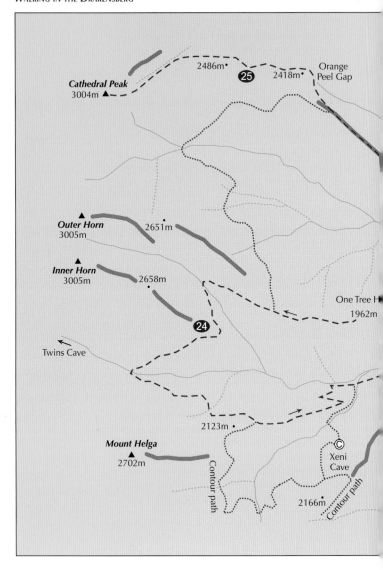

Cathedral Peak
3004m ▲

2486m•

25

2418m•

Orange
Peel Gap

Outer Horn ▲
3005m

2651m•

Inner Horn ▲
3005m

2658m
•

24

One Tree H
1962m

Twins Cave

2123m•

Mount Helga ▲
2702m

Contour path

Xeni
Cave
ⓒ

2166m•

Contour path

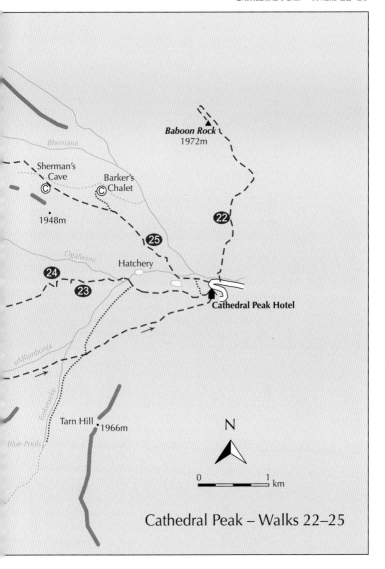

Cathedral Peak – Walks 22–25

Baboon Rock from Cathedral Peak Hotel

becomes steep, with steps and a mild scramble. There is a lull in the gradient but it is only to allow respiratory recovery before the next steep bit.

The way now leads round to the R (N) of the base of **Baboon Rock** summit, with a deep wooded valley to the R and precipitous cliffs falling away from the now very narrow path. ◄ The traverse of this slope which is mercifully level takes you well past the summit so it is necessary to turn up L to the ridge and then reverse course 180°. At this point the ridge is broad enough for relaxation, but there are big drops on either side, so if the grass is wet don't stray from the path. Just when you seem to have cracked it and the top must be oh so close, suddenly you come upon a distinctly narrow rock step down into a gap. There is big exposure here. It requires something of a head for heights, great care and the commonsense tactic of going no further if the rock is wet. Just beyond is the comfortable top, a great viewpoint. There is also the comfortable thought that the rock step is easier to get up than it was to go down if you had found it awkward.

Fortunately the convex slope conceals the drop. It is a time for great care and concentration.

WALK 23
One Tree Hill

Start	The sundial in Cathedral Peak Hotel
Distance	8km
Ascent	500m
Grade	Moderate
Time	3hrs 30mins

Summits are important to some people as an end point to a walk. Although this one is in itself unimpressive the walk up to it is a good one and the views excellent. It has the added advantage of not taking too long. It is a there-and-back affair. You can visit this top on Walk 24 if you prefer a bigger challenge.

From the sundial follow the corridor of rooms 15–41 and emerge from the accommodation by a signpost. Go straight ahead and ignore R forks to Cathedral Peak (300m) and Lake Jarred (500m), following pointers towards the 'Fern Forest'. Descend to cross the river, usually comfortably achieved at the weir above the **trout hatchery**. Remember, after significant rainfall this river may be not just dangerous but impossible to cross – a long diversion is possible via the Indiana Jones suspension bridge (see Walk 22) down near the golf course, but that's awfully tedious.

Let's assume you're across, possibly even with dryish feet. The path leads you to another 'Fern Forest' sign directing you upstream, soon to cross the smaller **Ogalweni** stream. At a stone cairn turn sharply L and uphill. A well-graded zig-zag path goes up to the NE ridge of the mountain, looking down into the uMlambonja valley. After this the path drifts back around to the N side of the ridge with occasional forays back up to peer over the edge. Bypass a large rocky band on its R side and reach the grassy **summit** plateau. Here the path goes

Approaching the top of One Tree Hill

In mist the precise summit may be difficult to locate.

steadfastly SW and bypasses the summit so you have to guess where precisely the top is. Head off L to the highest point visible, marked by a pathetically small pile of stones. ◄ Before you ask, yes, there once was a tree but it is long gone. Return the same way.

WALK 24

*One Tree Hill and the Contour Path
into the Mlambonja valley*

Start	The sundial in Cathedral Peak Hotel
Distance	21km
Ascent	900m
Grade	Strenuous
Time	8hrs

Quite a big and lonely circuit expedition for a day but in simply spectacular surroundings. Highly recommended for the fit and energetic.

Use the route for Walk 23 on the path that by-passes **One Tree Hill**, although a summit visit is clearly an option and takes only a few minutes. It doesn't look far up W to the readily visible **Contour Path** from here but this is deceptive, it is actually over 2km and almost 200m of climb. There is no signpost when you reach there but your way is L (NW). Lose a little height walking into the valley that runs down from between the Inner (L) and Outer (R) Horns, the two massive blocks that are above on the R. It is almost another 2km to the point where you turn SSE, cross the **stream** and return along the opposite side of the valley. This is what is challenging about the Contour Path in any part of the Drakensberg. Because it more or less follows the contours it needs to wind in and out of re-entrants without too much height loss or gain. That means much longer distances than a superficial glance at the KZNW map suggests and it is extraordinarily frustrating to see your path just across the valley, seemingly within touching distance, only for it to take a kilometre or even more to get there.

After crossing the **stream** at the end of the dog-leg mentioned above there's a bit of height gain before crossing a spur and starting the next foray into a deep re-entrant. This one is different. It is a bit wider than the last and is important for the adventurous fraternity who want to make the steep and awkward ascent up to Twins Cave and thereafter use the Mlambonja Pass to attain the Escarpment, a route not included here. The stream in this re-entrant is the infant uMlambonja and you'll meet it again later in the day. ▶ The problem is that the path disappears here, or at least it had at the time of writing. A trace of a path seemed to go down close to the stream and, although that direction seemed counter-intuitive, a bit of detective work then revealed the occasional cairn downstream which, when followed with diligence, led to a tiny and overgrown path going in what appeared to be the correct direction. The vegetation is just about penetrable and to begin with it is hard going. Zig-zags gain height leading to yet another spur to cross into a small re-entrant with a stream.

It is a good place for a picnic on a nice day, or indeed a camp if you are ever on a longer journey.

The Contour Path below the Outer and Inner Horns

This pattern is repeated a little further on but into a much wider and more mellow valley. Soon afterwards the **junction** where you leave the Contour Path heaves into sight, unsignposted, heralding the beginning of what will be a fairly long descent. Down **the shoulder of Mount Helga** you go, heading E, and where the ridge becomes much narrower some zig-zags lead down onto the floor of the now-familiar **uMlambonja** valley. At the bottom turn R (E) and follow a small path on the S side of the river for c800m and join the **Xeni Cave path** (Walk 18) at a SP (c1650m).

After a river crossing the path undulates all the way to the **crossing of the Tseketseke** stream. Go straight up the opposite bank and on to a **crossroads** with a triangular signpost stone: go straight over, uphill for a while and, unexpectedly if you haven't been this way before, you arrive on a football field. In the unlikely event that a match is in progress keep to the L touchline. Find the path on the L of the goalpost at the far end, which runs down towards the helipad, behind the house, then down the road to the hotel.

WALK 25
Cathedral Peak (3004m)

Start	The hotel sundial or, for visitors, the corner of the hairpin bend in the road immediately below Cathedral Peak Hotel
Distance	19km
Ascent	1600m
Grade	Strenuous (E, L)
Time	9–10 hrs

This is the classic route of the area, strenuous but without difficulty until tackling the face at the very end. There, the sections of scrambling, some with fixed aids, are very exposed. If you don't know the route on the final face it is difficult to find. For this reason a guide (available at Cathedral Peak Hotel) is recommended for first timers. In wet weather this section is very unsafe.

Visitors start at 1450m at the roadside signpost. Walk up the track W on the S bank of the stream for 400m to the **trout hatchery**. Those starting from the hotel tend to leave as for Walk 23 and turn R at the SP after 300m, leading down to join the main route.

Stone and wooden SPs on the track direct you R down a very small path to the **stream** which you cross to the N bank with another branch to cross immediately afterwards. At times of high water it may be necessary to cross using the bridge near the golf course (Walk 22).

The path climbs gently through grassland, crossing two mountain bike tracks and always aiming at the buttress of Bayman Hill (unnamed on map). Soon the gradient steepens, tempered by a few zig-zags, and turns the sandstone hill R gaining height all the time. Off to the R you can see Baboon Rock, and Ganapu Ridge rises towards the W. This is easier ground with a valley down to your R. A small **path** (2km from the start) leads

Approaching Bugger Gully below Cathedral Peak

R to Barker's Chalet, a grandiose name for a cave, even such a nice one with water close by. After a further 1km **Sherman's Cave** lies just above you on the L, another overhang with sleeping places. At the top of the valley the path crosses the **stream** to its N bank and goes up past a small waterfall to a flat area by the stream (c1890m). ◄

This is an important landmark as the last water supply on the route.

You are now on the grassland of the Little Berg. Steadily at first, then very steeply up the hill (locally known as 'Swine Hill' because it is) you reach a viewpoint on a **ridge** that the route follows for some 1.5km. At c2120m the start of the **Contour Path** leaves the route L. A very steep section precedes a sharp turn to the R to round a buttress, followed by a slight descent with some exposure down to the valley below on your R. Then up L is the dank, and in the mornings gloomy, loose rock ascent of a gully, taking you up to **Orange Peel Gap** (c2360m). ◄ A short ascent and then a long stretch, some 40 minutes' worth, of fairly level ground follows, with the ridge above you on the L.

This is another good rest place and is said to be the point where guides handed out oranges to their clients – a tradition that needs reinstating.

A valley rises up to meet you on the R, sadly with no stream (usually), and the point of intersection marks the start of 'Bugger Gully'. The name is self-explanatory and the ascent through boulders is tiresome. At last you reach the final wall of **Cathedral Peak** and the excitement begins. The face is very steep and the usual route has significant exposure. There are seven defined scrambling sections including a chain ladder pitch. It takes about an hour to reach the summit from the foot of the face. ◄

Return the same way.

MONK'S COWL (1480M)

The needle top of Amphlett's with Turret to its L

As you approach Monk's Cowl you know straight away that you are in the close company of big mountains. Invariably it is the sturdy, flat-topped Cathkin Peak (3149m: in Zulu, 'Mdedelelo') that catches the eye. On closer inspection from the Reserve main gate you see to its right the spiky Sterkhorn (2973m), then further right again the smaller but rather obviously named 'Turret' and then Amphletts' (2620m). Behind them on the R are the jagged points of the Dragon's Back, running down N from the plateau.

The peak of Monk's Cowl itself (3229m) is hidden behind Cathkin Peak. Both are serious climbs. Champagne Castle, at 3246m the third highest peak in the Drakensberg, is a shallow dome and lies south of Monk's Cowl. It is more or less part of the escarpment as well as being invisible from the entrance to the Reserve. One of the stories relating to its naming is that the celebratory bottle of champagne had a fatal accident before opening after the first successful ascent. The mountain is easily ascended from the Little Berg, an arduous and long walk via Gray's Pass. It really isn't a day trip.

There are **four** start points for walks in this section. The first is the KZN Wildlife Office and the second the Champagne Castle Hotel, a bit further east along the road in. Walk 33 is a linear walk back from Injisuthi camp, to which your hotel will be able to give you a lift and Walks 35 and 36 set out from the Drakensberg Sun Hotel, which is just outside the park, to the north (see directions in the 'Getting There' section overleaf).

GETTING THERE

From OR Tambo International Airport, Johannesburg
Follow the N3 (SP Durban) to exit 230, turning E on N11 towards Ladysmith. After about 6km turn R onto R600 (SP Winterton) and continue back over the N3 to reach Winterton itself. The R600 leads round the E side of the town and goes R at the traffic lights. Cross the bridge and continue 35km to Monk's Cowl.

From King Shaka International Airport, Durban
Leave the airport via the connection to the N2, the main N–S coastal route. Drive S for about 30km to the interchange with the N3 (SP Pietermaritzburg). Once established on the N3 heading N continue until you pass W of Estcourt. Take exit 179 and turn L (SP Loskop). After 24km go through Loskop village; another 6km brings you to the crossroads with R600. Turn L and drive for almost 20km to the Park entrance and Champagne Castle Hotel.

For the Drakensberg Sun Hotel, follow R600 and pass Cedarwood Shopping Centre (R) and the Champagne Sports Resort (L). Soon afterwards there is a road junction where the main road to Monk's Cowl reserve goes straight on. Turn R here (SP) and the Sun is at the end of the road.

FACILITIES

Winterton has an ATM, Post Office, pharmacy, supermarket and petrol. Estcourt is larger but with similar facilities.

There is ample accommodation outside the Park within easy distance. This is the Champagne Valley and there is a big choice of every kind of establishment from simple B&B accommodation to large hotels, notably Champagne Castle (www.champagnecastle.co.za) and the Drakensberg Sun (www.southernsun.com).

There is a small shopping centre (Cedarwood) with a supermarket, bottle store and craft shops 10km from the Park entrance on R600 at a road junction opposite Champagne Sports Resort. Within the Park there is only a small campsite with a café at the KZN Wildlife HQ but no provisions or other facilities.

MAP REQUIRED

KZN Wildlife uKhahlamba-Drakensberg Park Hiking Map 2

WALK 26
Nandi's Falls

Start	Reserve entrance
Distance	8km
Ascent	250m
Grade	Easy
Time	2hrs 30mins

A pleasant and straightforward walk to an enchanting waterfall, almost a secret place.

Start at **Monk's Cowl main gate**, turn R immediately and go down past the buildings to a stone SP, numbered 1 (note that not all SPs are numbered). Follow the direction for Sterkspruit Falls. The path winds down easily through woodland, eventually onto open ground and down to a SP. Turn L (SP uMakhulumane Rock) and continue down through a gate in a fence. After about 150m there is another SP indicating a L turn for Nandi's Falls. The next SP also directs you L for the Falls and just 60m later again keep L at a stone SP (to the R here lies the path for walk 37, uMakhulumane Rock, and walk 27, Hlathikulu Forest).

Cross two small streams on rustic bridges, the path then settling down in the ever-narrowing valley of the **Sterkspruit stream** which is down to your R. Later, ignore the wooden sign and path R for 'Pools' and keep to the main path, up steeply at times, to reach a SP (no.5) that reveals the suggested return route up L ('Office'). Here go R, quickly down to yet another SP (R for Hlathikulu Forest) after which a sometimes rocky and undulating way leads you to your final route choice. Try to ignore the tempting path down R to the stream and instead walk bravely into the shady forest ahead. Any of the many little tracks therein will take you in a few metres to **Nandi's Falls**.

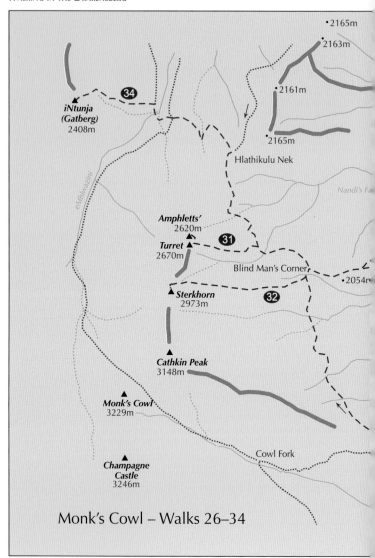

• 2165m

• 2163m

• 2161m

34

▲ **iNtunja**
(Gatberg)
2408m

• 2165m

Hlathikulu Nek

Nandi's Fa

eMhlwazini

Amphletts'
2620m

Turret ▲ **31**
2670m

Blind Man's Corner

• 2054n

▲ **Sterkhorn**
2973m

32

▲ **Cathkin Peak**
3148m

▲ **Monk's Cowl**
3229m

Cowl Fork

▲ **Champagne**
Castle
3246m

Monk's Cowl – Walks 26–34

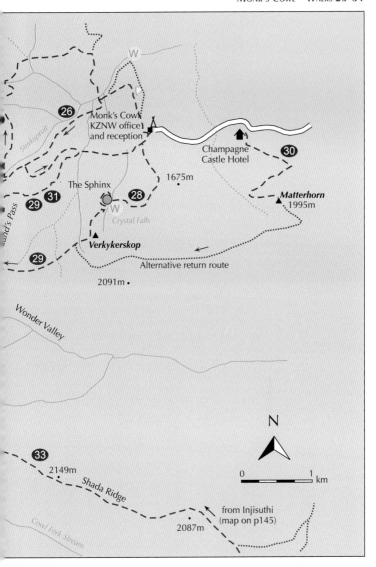

26

Monk's Cowl
KZNW office
and reception

Sterkspruit

Champagne
Castle Hotel

30

1675m

The Sphinx

29 31

28

Matterhorn
1995m

Crystal Falls

nd's Pass

Verkykerskop

29

Alternative return route

2091m

Wonder Valley

N

33

2149m

Shada Ridge

0   1
km

from Injisuthi
(map on p145)

2087m

Cowl Fork Stream

119

Nandi's Falls

For the return journey retrace your steps to SP5 and turn R. This climbs steadily but easily and passes two signs indicating the route to Keartland's Pass. At the second of these you pick up the route for Walk 29 which takes you back to the car park. Less interesting is to retrace your steps.

WALK 27

Hlathikulu Forest

Start	Reserve entrance
Distance	9km
Ascent	400m
Grade	Easy
Time	3hrs 30mins

Hlathikulu is a Zulu word meaning tall trees. This is a pleasant little walk through open country, plunging into a world of Yellowwoods and, in spring, birdsong. Indeed, this is a highly recommended walk for birders where local 'specials' can be seen. The short detour to Nandi's Falls should be considered mandatory (see Walk 26).

Leave **Monk's Cowl main gate** and follow the route for Walk 26 until the path signed for Makhulumane Rock and Hlathikulu Forest breaks R. Go down and cross the small stream and then the **Sterkspruit stream** followed by a fairly steep climb to reach a path junction.

Turn L as indicated on a wooden SP. The path goes uphill for a short distance before levelling off and soon entering quite thick woodland with a lot of undergrowth. The path continues to undulate across the hillside and traverses another significant area of woodland before eventually going back down to the **Sterkspruit stream**. After crossing you need to go downstream for a few metres to find the path up the other side, where it arrives at a junction. For Nandi's Falls turn R (Walk 26). For home turn L then R at the next SP. From here climb steadily but easily up, past the first and second signs on the R for Keartland's Pass, drop down across the stream (a good birding area), and follow the undulating route to the car-park.

WALK 28
Crystal Falls, the Sphinx and Verkykerskop

Start	Reserve entrance
Distance	4.5km, 5.5km, 7km
Ascent	260m, 300m, 520m
Grade	Easy
Time	1hr 30mins, 2hrs, 3hrs

A shortish walk to a waterfall, slightly further to a viewpoint, and further still to a proper top with a good view of the Little Berg and mountains beyond.

Although not particularly spectacular it is a nice enough waterfall to sit by, and a good end point (also known as a bribe) for a child's outing.

Leave the Monk's Cowl main gate and go through the gate and straight ahead. After 100m turn L at the signpost for Crystal Falls. The way is steep and wooded. After c700m cross a stream and arrive at a crossroads which is unmarked on the map. Go straight over. The path is easy to follow and well graded, describing an arc to the S and W. At c1680m a path joins L direct from Champagne Castle Hotel and soon after that there is a L fork for the sunken forest which, for today's walk, can be ignored. **Crystal Falls** is on the L in a grove of trees just after this at c1750m and about 2km from the start. ◄

Leave the waterfall on the same good path, rising only gently, for a further 500m, which takes you round a L-hand bend under the alleged face of the **Sphinx**. It is easy and quick to follow the path up and round the back to the top, and this is a good and safe place to sit and admire the views.

Verkykerskop from Breakfast Stream

If you feel the urge to go further there's a good little challenge not far ahead which is still only a walk, although the finish is admittedly a bit 'nose-to-ground'. Keep on following the same path which zig-zags off to the S before resuming its SW line and reaching the grassland of the Little Berg. On the L and just behind as you arrive in a small clump of trees is a clear but appallingly steep little path which leads mercifully quickly to the top of a cone-shaped hill called **Verkykerskop**. It is only a 70m ascent to the grassy top with a large boulder, which brings a fine if strenuous finish to the jaunt. Verkykerskop is an Afrikaans name meaning a place where you can look out over the terrain. It would probably be called 'Spyglass Hill' in the novels I read as a child, but we'll stick with the original. Return the same way.

WALK 29
Blind Man's Corner and return via Keartland's Pass

Start	Reserve entrance
Distance	12.5km
Ascent	700m
Grade	Moderate
Time	4hrs

A scenic round trip up onto the Little Berg, with a little-used route for the return journey.

You can take in **Crystal Falls** and the **Sphinx** on the way as you follow the route for Walk 28 to the base of **Verkykerskop**, the point at which you reach the Little Berg. Just ahead lies the descriptively-named 'Breakfast stream' at c1945m. Refresh yourself here, then cross the

The important path junction of Blindman's Corner with Cathkin Peak behind

stream and head off W across the grassland. This is great walking country and you will make fast progress, with the Sterkhorn directly in front and Cathkin Peak just away to the L.

With just 500m to go before reaching **Blind Man's Corner** note the way back down Keartland's Pass leaving R. A slight rise in the ground brings you to your clearly-signposted destination (c2080m) at a junction with the **contour path**, an important traffic intersection in this part of the Drakensberg. To the L (S and then SE) it leads via Shada Ridge eventually to Injisuthi (see Walk 33). To the R (NW and later W) it is the only way, if a circuitous one, over to the Cathedral Peak area. This is an opportunity to sit at the foot of the Sterkhorn and assess the best line for a future climb (see Walk 32).

For the return trip, go back to the SP for **Keartland's Pass** and fork L. One of the tributaries of the Sterkspruit plunges down NE into a wide and deep valley as it descends from the plateau and it is into this that the path leads, corkscrewing steeply down the E side. Lower down go round a corner R and under a wondrously weathered mushroom of sandstone into a shady grove of trees with a stream (c1740m). After a short level stretch another stream/trees combination appears and then the path starts to lose height again.

Ultimately there is a steep descent down an obvious but short and narrow spur, passing en route a side path with a warning to 'keep out' or take your chance with 'vicious dogs', a friendly sort of greeting to travellers or perhaps just the unadorned truth. Keep R and go down to join the **path** from Nandi Falls at c1550m, over the **stream** and tediously up the other side. From here you can see the car park but just as you think it is all over there is a veritable switchback to challenge tired legs.

WALK 30
Matterhorn (1995m)

Start	Champagne Castle Hotel
Distance	5km
Ascent	450m
Grade	Moderate (E)
Time	2hrs 30mins

The house peak of Champagne Castle Hotel. A short climb leads to a wonderful summit on the Little Berg with no technical difficulties but some exposure on a very narrow path. Some of the walk crosses private land and is accessed through the Hotel grounds, so if you are not staying at the Hotel it would be appropriate to ask permission at Reception.

Leave the Hotel Reception to go up past the bowling green and cross over the track at the top onto a small path. The signpost is for 'Sunset Trail'. Wind up past the observation tower and come to a path junction. Fork R, again signed

'Sunset Trail'. The path climbs steadily up the open hillside SE of the hotel. At about the halfway mark (in time) you cross a small stream in a pleasant, shady grove of trees. ◄ Soon after this the path steepens dramatically and becomes rocky, gaining height very quickly.

There now follows a stretch of some 200m length along a narrow balcony with some significant exposure on your R. Care in foot placement is important here to avoid the odd stone and the wooden posts that help support the path, as these are often hidden by long grass. After this the path becomes steep again and turns E to take you up the final easy slopes of the **Matterhorn** to the comfortable top, a marvellous viewpoint.

Using the same route for descent you will be down again in an hour or less. An alternative is to cross the Little Berg following a small path, or in some places small cairns, which brings you out between **Verkykerskop** (see Walk 28) and the Breakfast stream, from where you return via the **Sphinx** and **Crystal Falls**. ◄ Allow an extra hour and a half for this variation.

This is a good place to replenish your water supplies.

The final section of this offers a really good chance of seeing Mountain Reedbuck, especially in the early morning.

WALK 31
Amphletts' (2620m)

Start	Reserve entrance
Distance	18km
Ascent	1200m
Grade	Strenuous (**T**)
Time	7–8hrs

An infrequently climbed rocky peak, generally straightforward but with one slightly exposed and awkward passage lower down. The small path only appears higher up the route.

Follow the route for Walk 29 and as you cross the Little Berg towards **Blind Man's Corner** identify the ridge that you will use for ascent. Turn R and go along the **Contour Path** to the first **stream** (just under 1km). About 300m after this take to the hillside, usually trackless. Go up L to the grassy crest above and follow it L until you are on the edge of a ridge leading up W to the peak. A faint path appears. Go up along the edge until it becomes rockier and steeper. Here find a small traverse line, slightly precarious and hazardous when wet, going into the deep gully on your L.

Ascend the gully without difficulty until a line of rocks, coming down from the summit, appears on your R. Climb these until you can make your way on a path around the E side of the peak as far as a point just N of the **summit**. You can stop here or scale the none-too-difficult rocks to the real top. Return the same way.

WALK 32

Sterkhorn (2973m)

Start	Reserve entrance
Distance	17km
Ascent	1550m
Grade	Strenuous (**E**)
Time	7hrs

A serious mountain walk which should not be underestimated. Good weather is crucial to success, as is a tolerance of some exposure. In places the route is hideously steep. On the credit side there are no technical climbing problems. The mountain is also known as 'Mount Memory' to commemorate those South Africans who died in WW2 but locally the name has never caught on.

Local opinion is that if you don't have experience of the route you should hire a community guide, irrespective of your mountaineering expertise.

The hideously steep path at the beginning of the Sterkhorn climb

Use the route for Walk 29 to reach **Blind Man's Corner**. Turn L as for Injisuthi and quickly reach a grove of trees which conceals a tiny stream. On emerging from this area immediately turn up the hill following an obvious small path in the grassland which runs almost due west: the route starts by following the edge of the E ridge of the mountain. There is no messing about with wimpish zig-zags. ▶ In places there are very short sections of rocky scrambles but they are energy-draining rather than difficult.

Still on the edge of the E ridge, when the gradient eases on the grassland you are confronted with a very narrow section, considerably exposed on either side. It is quite short but in very windy conditions or with mud, sometimes frozen, on the narrow path even more care is required. This brings you out under a rocky buttress (c2515m) which you round on its R side along narrow ledges, again quite exposed. The ledges take you above the buttress but still on the ridge edge. Now the tiny path, mostly easy to follow, slants R across the face of the mountain, encountering yet another rock barrier a little higher. As before, you round this on the R,

It is dead straight and in places fiercely steep – as one observer put it 'it is like going up the side of a house'.

Cathkin Peak and Sterkhorn (R) seen from below Verkykerskop

on a ledge which is mildly precarious. Above this you emerge on steep grassland and you will love the final very steep ascent in a direct line, aiming for the deep rock niche above. The final few metres are very eroded and awkward, consisting of earth or mud, frozen in winter: the main safety features are handfuls of grass and divine providence.

Ahead is a vertiginous drop down into the eMhlwazini valley.

On arriving at the niche there is a comfortable place to sit and leave the rucksacks. ◄ The next bit is 'interesting'. Scramble up easy rock by the stance in the direction of the E face of the mountain. Continue around this face on easy ground until the way ahead appears impassable. Look R and there is a narrow cleft: a difficult climb. But underneath is a small cave. Crawl in (honestly!). Light appears above and you exit vertically onto a very safe platform. This is why you must leave your rucksack below and why, how shall we say – those of more ample waistline – may struggle. There remains just some additional easy scrambling, mildly exposed, to reach the cairn and white cross at the spacious summit. Return the same way.

WALK 33

Injisuthi to Monk's Cowl via Van Heyningen's Pass

Start	Injisuthi camp
Distance	21km
Ascent	750m
Grade	Strenuous
Time	6hrs 30mins

One of the best long walks in the Drakensberg, incorporating the clever Van Heyningen's Pass and astonishing views of big mountains. The only drawback as a day walk is the requirement to be dropped off at Injisuthi in the morning. Hotels can usually arrange this.

Use the route to Walk 39 to reach the viewpoint above **Van Heyningen's Pass**. Here there is a 90° turn and you head NW across open grassland dotted with occasional *Protea* trees, gaining about 100m in height to a floor-level signpost at a path junction c1940m. Turn L (erroneously) marked 'Contour path' (you will actually meet that some way ahead). The way is always comfortable, an encouraging feature of the whole route, keeping the deep valley of Cowl Fork below your L hip and slightly higher ground to your R. A faint track (no SP) comes in from the R just as you get onto **Shada Ridge** at c2020m. You round **pt2087m** on its N side just a few metres below it, and after swerving W across the broad ridge, resume an almost NW direction, gaining height slowly as you progress. ▶

After a little burst of uphill work you reach the rather vague junction with the **Contour Path** at c2180m. Turn R and simply follow this all the way down to **Blind Man's Corner**. On this section you run almost parallel with the 2200m contour line for a while so there is a fairly sharp descent in the final third. Also, as well as noting the

The Contour Path from Shada Ridge approaching Blind Man's Corner

At this stage you are heading directly towards the E ridge of Cathkin Peak.

131

eye-catching pattern of shadows reaching down into the depths of Wonder Valley on your R, you will cross several re-entrants. The last of these before you reach Blind Man's Corner is particularly pleasant and, although it hasn't the cachet of a name, it is a much better stopping place than the famous Corner ahead.

To finish the trip to Monk's Cowl go down past **Verkykerskop** (Walk 28) or the longer and harder **Keartland's Pass** (Walk 29).

WALK 34
iNtunja/Gatberg (2408m)

Start	Reserve entrance
Distance	26km
Ascent	1400m
Grade	Strenuous (**E**)
Time	9–10hrs

The Zulu word 'iNtunja' means 'a hole', rather non-specifically. This walk makes for an interesting but physically demanding day trip. Although the summit itself just needs care, the visit to the 9m diameter hole mandates careful assessment of the risk involved.

Use the route for Walk 29 as far as **Blind Man's Corner**. Turn R along the **Contour Path** and at **Hlathikulu Nek** keep L to go gradually downhill for 1.2km to an unmarked crossroads c1996m. To the L is the route to the Keith Bush campsite and Gray's Pass. Half-right is a tiny track down the spur to reach Zulu Cave. Your path is straight on and downhill to the **eMhlwazini** stream at c1900m. Cross and play a bit of hide and seek on the other bank looking for the continuation of the Contour Path. When you find it walk downstream for c150m, always looking up L for the

iNtunja (Gatberg) –
the path follows the
righthand grassy ridge

direct path to iNtunja. It helps to have identified the correct line beforehand as you descend the path to the river.

The route now takes you in steep steps interspersed
with some more level sections up an increasingly narrow and rocky ridge. There is one steep and exposed step
with a big drop L which needs care on the return journey.
Eventually crest the top of the ridge and turn W, the path
being awkward to follow in places.

To get to the 'hole', go L and across the E face of the
summit rocks, hugging the rock wall. The small path is a
very narrow, very exposed and very precarious. Indeed,
you should think carefully before proceeding, particularly after rain.

For the **summit** climb go round to the NW side and
you will find evidence of the route. It is a short scramble
but the rock is poor with few good handholds. It can be
daunting to many and demands care. The top is a small,
flat, narrow grassy area. Return the same way.

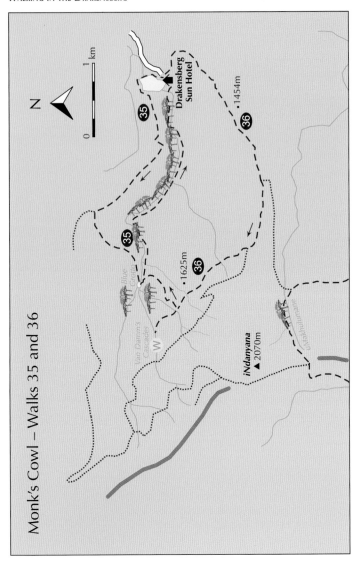

Monk's Cowl – Walks 35 and 36

WALK 35

Blue Grotto

Start	Drakensberg Sun Hotel
Distance	6.5km
Ascent	320m
Grade	Easy
Time	2hrs 30mins

The walk is described anti-clockwise, the most interesting way of doing it. An easier option would be to go along the river, that is clockwise, as far as the grotto and then reverse your steps to return. However, younger children might still struggle with the undulating nature of this path.

GETTING TO THE DRAKENSBERG SUN HOTEL

Follow R600 and pass Cedarwood Shopping centre on the R and the Champagne Sports Resort on the L. Just afterwards there is a fork in the road, the main road to the Park gate going L. Turn R here (SP for the hotel) and the Sun is at the end of the road.

Leave at the rear of the Drakensberg Sun Hotel going R in the direction of the stables, first crossing the dam wall. Go through the stable entrance barrier where there is a SP. The dirt road goes uphill past houses and soon there is another SP for your destination: don't go R which is for 'Fern Forest'. From here on you are on a path rather than anything bigger, and soon you reach woodland, taking the L fork when you reach a junction.

You will pass the turn-off for Barry's grave on the R. This commemorates a young climber who was killed on Monk's Cowl in 1938. The final section down to the **grotto** is very steep and involves steps. You arrive in a cave after crossing a small water-course on stepping stones. Keep going and you will see the lovely (and sometimes blue) pool fed by a waterfall.

Leave the grotto by crossing the exit stream to the R bank and following the narrow path at some height above the stream, initially at least. Almost immediately note the turning up R towards Van Damm's Cascades, which is not marked on the KZNW map. Keep on the main path, which leads through woodland for almost the entire course back to the Hotel and is way-marked in blue. Generally the way is undulating; up and down steps occasionally but always close to the river with its small falls and pools. ◄ Be careful not to miss the **river crossing** by a 'Grotto' sign about three quarters of the way down; if you do miss the turn you will reach an obvious dead end some 50m further on, and should retrace your steps. At a T-junction near the end of the route turn R across the bridge and then follow the obvious last section to the Hotel.

It might be described as gloomy by some or enchanting by others but never lacking in interest. Mosses and lichens abound.

WALK 36
Van Damm's Cascades

Start	Drakensberg Sun Hotel
Distance	12km
Ascent	550m
Grade	Moderate
Time	4hrs 30mins

An outing of great diversity of surroundings; from wide open grassland to narrow, wooded river gorges. Not too far, never too steep, never uninteresting.

Leave up the hotel drive and go R through the security barrier of the housing complex. Remember to pay your Park fees and sign the hiker's register before leaving. A yellow trail sign directs you around the inner fencing but no-one seems to mind if you march quietly and purposefully up Yellowwood Road, steeply at times, until you branch L after passing House No.22 following a sign for Cleo's Pool. ▶ After a little under 3km of walking more or less in a straight line, the path for Cleo's Pool goes left. Ignore that and continue more steeply to a fence line by a small rocky barrier. This is the Park boundary (c1540m). Go through the barrier and walk up to a path junction indicating L for uMakhulumane Rock (which also leads to the Monk's Cowl office) and R for Van Damm's cascades.

This path leads across fairly level open grassland with fine views to the mountains ahead and to the left.

A few metres further on a small path breaks off L for the Steilberg but you keep straight on. This is easy going again across open grassland heading NW. A good indicator to look out for is an inverted triangle of trees hanging down from the Little Berg. When you reach this you have to cross the expected and inevitable stream but, more importantly, immediately beforehand take note of a small and unmarked **path** off to the R. This is your descent path for the return journey and it is unmarked on the KZNW map.

Continue over the **stream**, again keeping fairly level, and very quickly you will reach the bottom of the promised **cascades**. They are a pleasant sight when there is decent water flow, but much less impressive in the dry times of mid-winter. But it is the whole walk, not just the cascades that you've set out for. ▶

Look out for the baboon troop commonly seen here.

Now retrace your steps for the short distance to the stream mentioned above where, after crossing, turn L down the very small, un-signposted path noted earlier. Although at first slightly uphill it soon descends very steeply through *Protea* trees. At c1490m you go out through the Park boundary fence, a tight fit but blame your backpack, immediately crossing a small stream.

Now it is back to open grassland, through a small thicket and a slightly uphill march with the deep tree-filled valley steeply below you. After a short level section suddenly the path plunges very steeply down L almost to river level. Here, at a T-junction, you meet the **Blue Grotto route**, the grotto being only a few metres to your L and really well worth a visit. To get home follow the directions from here given in Walk 35.

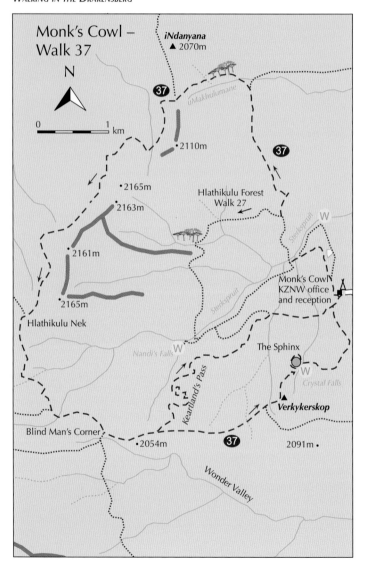

Monk's Cowl –
Walk 37

N

0 _____ 1 km

iNdanyana
▲ 2070m

37

uMakholumane

•2110m

•2165m

•2163m

Hlathikulu Forest
Walk 27

37

Sterkspruit

W

•2161m

Monk's Cowl
KZNW office
and reception

•2165m

Sterkspruit

Hlathikulu Nek

Nandi's Falls

W

The Sphinx

W

Crystal Falls

Keartland's Pass

Verkykerskop

Blind Man's Corner

•2054m

37

2091m •

Wonder Valley

WALK 37

*uMakhulumane Stream, the Little Berg
and Hlathikulu Nek – The smugglers' path*

Start	Reserve entrance
Distance	21km
Ascent	850m
Grade	Strenuous
Time	8hrs

A big, remote, but hugely enjoyable outing with no route-finding difficulties. The originally awkward section at the top of the uMakhulumane forest now has a ladder and the walk is open again. However, it is still used by Basotho smugglers, usually nocturnally, and further deterioration is possible. Enquire at the Monk's Cowl office before you start.

Leave **Monk's Cowl main gate** and follow Walk 26 as far as the turn-off R for uMakhulumane Rock. Go down and cross the small stream and then the **Sterkspruit stream**, followed by a fairly steep climb, eventually arriving at a path junction and SP.

Keep straight on here towards uMakhulumane Rock. Follow the undulating path across pleasant hillside for a little over 2km before reaching a stile (c1600m). Just over 100m past the stile is another **path junction**. Keep L uphill and then dive down into the woodland that surrounds the **uMakhulumane stream** (the R fork turns sharply E towards the Drakensberg Sun hotel and meets Walk 36 at the bottom of the Steilberg).

The path in this somewhat gloomy forest climbs steeply all the way up to the open area of the Little Berg. The path is generally easy to follow but the exit from the forest up to the R was originally very tricky. The path had crumbled away leaving an unholy combination of steep earth, mud, grass and loose rocks: not even a decent tree root for a handhold. However, once this section of some

The circle marks the ladders as you leave the uMakhulumane Forest

Off to the W is the extraordinary peak called iNtunja (or Gatberg, see Walk 34) with the remarkable hole of some 9m diameter.

5m has been surmounted, hopefully with a ladder, you've cracked it.

Go round a rock buttress and down into the gloom of some trees by two waterfalls. The path leads through these and up onto the open grassland above. It ascends very steeply to the crest which is marked by a number of small boulders. As soon as you reach this point (c2015m) the crest path is immediately in front of you.

This crest path is easy to follow. Where you join it its direction is E–W but this is just a kink and it quickly resumes a generally N–S line. You are on the W side of the tops now and stay there all the way to Hlathikulu Nek (c2095m), a distance of about 5.4km of easy, fast walking. You would expect to see a path junction before reaching the halfway point, a subsidiary route heading NW towards Eagle Gorge, but we saw no sign of it. ◀

It is mildly uphill just before the path junction that is the **Nek** and after all your efforts thus far this can hurt a bit. From the Nek follow the easy contour path SE for 3km down to **Blind Man's Corner** and return from there using Walk 29 initially and then either carry straight on to follow Walk 28 (fastest) or fork left to follow Walk 29 (most interesting).

INJISUTHI (1470M)

Marble Baths

It is reasonable to call Injisuthi 'the hidden gem of the Drakensberg'. In fact it is not that well hidden but does lie 32km S of Loskop. Of this stretch of road the first 21km are surfaced but pothole-ridden and very populous, the next 4km are unsurfaced and the final 7km, within the Park boundary, are of respectable quality tar.

GETTING THERE

From OR Tambo International Airport, Johannesburg
Follow the N3 (SP Durban) to exit 230, turning E on the N11 towards Ladysmith. After about 6km turn R onto R600 (SP Winterton) and continue back over the N3 to reach Winterton itself. The R600 leads round the E side of the town and goes R at the traffic lights. Cross the bridge and drive for 14km to an obvious crossroads. Turn L (SP) and drive to the village of Loskop (no facilities). Turn R (S) at the SP for Injisuthi. The camp is 32km straight ahead.

From King Shaka International Airport, Durban
Leave the airport via the connection to the N2, the main N–S coastal route. Drive S for about 30km to the interchange with the N3 (SP Pietermaritzburg). Once established on the N3 heading N continue until you pass W of Estcourt. Take exit 179 and turn L (SP Loskop). After 24km reach Loskop village: turn L in the centre (SP) and drive for 32km to the Park HQ and camp reception.

FACILITIES

Winterton has an ATM, post office, pharmacy, supermarket and petrol. Estcourt is larger but with similar facilities.

The only accommodation S of Loskop lies within the Park. At Park HQ the rest camp is idyllically situated in a grove of plane trees by the side of the Delmhlwazini stream, with a large grassy area kept mown short and offering enormous opportunities for play. The chalets are basic but well-equipped, with gas for heating, cooking and refrigeration, and electricity from 5pm to 10pm but no power points. Chalets are serviced daily. The camp site is close by. There is a small shop in the camp office but only minimal basic supplies are available. There is no mobile phone signal.

MAPS REQUIRED

KZN Wildlife uKhahlamba-Drakensberg Park Hiking Maps 2 and 3

WALK 38

Poacher's Stream

Start	Road bridge 1km S of Injisuthi Camp
Distance	4.5km
Ascent	200m
Grade	Easy
Time	1hr 30mins

A short walk suitable for a picnic, or for a morning outing when the position of the sun gives terrific mountain views.

Walk or drive back down the camp approach road to the **bridge over the Njesuthi stream**. Continue down the road for 150m. A signposted path rises R to climb steeply between the rocks to more level grassland. You then go easily on a good path to **Poacher's Stream** where there are nice pools. Cross the stream and after climbing the bank you soon join the Battle Cave path (Walk 42). It is downhill from there, re-crossing Poacher's Stream just before reaching the Njesuthi at their **confluence**. ▶ On the opposite bank go R through woodland for 200m before zig-zagging to gain height, and after about 1km arriving back at the bridge.

This crossing may be awkward or impossible in summer.

Injisuthi camp

143

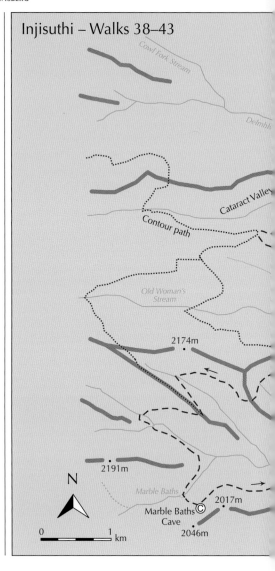

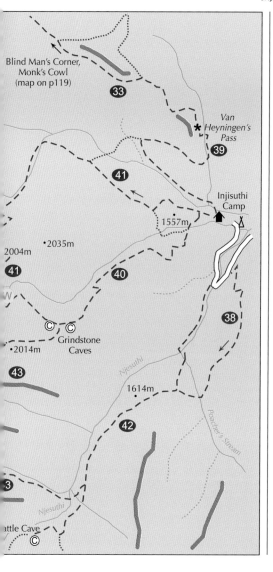

Blind Man's Corner,
Monk's Cowl
(map on p119)

33

*Van
Heyningen's
Pass*

★

39

41

Injisuthi
Camp

1557m

•2035m

2004m

41

40

38

W~

© ©
©
Grindstone
Caves

•2014m

43

•2014m

Njesuthi

1614m
•

42

Poacher's Stream

3

Njesuthi

attle Cave

©

WALK 39
Van Heyningen's Pass to the viewpoint

Start	Injisuthi Camp
Distance	8km
Ascent	350m
Grade	Easy
Time	3hrs

A fascinating walk up through the cleverly designed and historical pass to a great viewpoint. It also offers the opportunity to walk to the Monk's Cowl Reserve (see Walk 33).

Leave Injisuthi camp by the path which starts behind chalets 3 and 4 and cross the **river** on the footbridge. The path follows the N bank of the stream comfortably for 1.5km, finally rising more steeply to a SP. Turn R, back on yourself, and gain height steadily going generally E then SE until the path turns sharply N into a narrow wooded valley in which you cross its **stream** to the E bank. When you **re-cross** to the W bank higher up you are at c1680m. The cleverly-engineered path, named after the forester in charge of the Monk's Cowl Forest Station in the 1930s, winds up through nice woods until at c1750m you enter the dramatic defile of **Van Heyningen's Pass**, with towering sandstone blocks on either side. You emerge from this up on the Little Berg and, soon after a right-angle turn to the W, reach a marvellous viewpoint, the perfect stop for a drink and a deserved rest. ◄

You are looking up the Cowl Fork valley with jagged Monk's Cowl (3229m) perched dramatically between the flat blocks of Champagne Castle (L) and Cathkin Peak (R).

Unless you are continuing to Monk's Cowl the only return route is by the outward path.

WALK 40
Grindstone Caves

Start	Injisuthi Camp
Distance	7km
Ascent	400m
Grade	Easy
Time	3hrs

A locally popular walk to a well-used (and quite well hidden) backpacker's cave with its own reliable water supply.

Leave the camp at the signpost close to chalet 2. Walk steeply for 300m to a path junction. Turn L and after passing above the camp staff quarters go through the Yellowwood forest and cross **Old Woman Stream** by the bridge. After 30m there is another path junction where you turn L. The way ahead is easy, but steep, and you climb up towards an obvious sandstone buttress. The path then slips round to the R, and a slight descent onto flatter ground follows, with Old Woman Stream way below to your R. After climbing again the path runs just below a series of narrow

The well hidden Grindstone Cave

sandstone bands, and these provide a helpful landmark when the route is reversed (as in Walk 41).

The first, and larger, of the two **Grindstone caves** is in a corner and concealed by foliage. It lies close to the path, and one clue to its position is the sound of the year-round waterfall hidden inside. The second and much smaller cave lies a little further along the path, after the signed **junction** with the path going up onto the Little Berg (see Walk 43). Return the same way.

WALK 41
Cataract Valley

Start	Injisuthi Camp
Distance	12.5km
Ascent	600m
Grade	Moderate
Time	5–6hrs

One of the finest of the shorter walks of the Drakensberg. Great views, varied terrain and some minor navigational challenges make this a 'must-do' venture if you are in the area.

Leave the camp as for Walk 40 and go up to the first junction. Continue straight on (W) at an easier gradient. At 1km from the camp find another junction. Turn R (NW) here and continue for about 1.2km over easy grassland to yet another path junction. Continuing in the same line takes you downhill for 400m to cross the surprisingly small **Cataract Valley** stream.

Here the path veers SW uphill with the stream to your L and, apart from an exaggerated zig-zag of 100m or so, maintains the same course until the valley becomes extremely narrow. Here the path crosses the stream to the E bank only to re-cross within 40m. Just 250m on is the final **crossing** and from there you wind up the hillside turning sharply L (E) at one point (care needed: in long grass this turn is not obvious), resuming a westerly course after 300m. The view ahead, centred on Old Woman Grinding Corn (2986m), is outstanding. ▶

Soon you arrive at a signpost, the first of two closely-set **junctions**. Turn L (SP Grindstone Caves) and after 20m turn L again, climbing up to a shallow and unnamed col (c1990m) between the two **spot heights** of 2004m and 2035m. This is the highest point of the route.

The path leaves the col SW, soon turning S to cross a small stream in a shallow valley at the point where the water tumbles over the edge as a waterfall. Continue in the same line down the hillside towards Old Woman Stream. There is one zig-zag L followed by a less obvious one R. Missing this takes you too far L and in towards the waterfall in the corner. The correct line is upstream to cross **Old Woman Stream** above the obvious **waterfall** and not, as the KZNW map suggests, below it. On the opposite bank the very small path climbs steeply for a while but quickly settles

You are always likely to be alone hereabouts and that adds to the grandeur of the surroundings.

Old Woman Grinding Corn ahead as you climb out of Cataract Valley

down to contour at around 1860m for over 1km to reach **Grindstone Caves**.

Note that the hillside hereabouts is covered with small tracks, some vague, some encouraging, some human, some animal, but the trick is to keep high, referring both to the map and the details of Walk 40 to find the cave and the easiest way back to camp.

WALK 42
Battle Cave

Start	Road bridge 1km S of Injisuthi Camp
Distance	10km
Ascent	425m
Grade	Moderate
Time	4hrs

An easy walk through nice scenery to one of the great Bushman painting sites of the Drakensberg now decreed a National Monument. To access the cave you must take a local guide bookable at the camp office.

Walk or drive to the road bridge over the Njesuthi river. A signposted path climbs above the W bank of the river, descending to river level after 1km. A 200m walk through woodland leads to the point of crossing the Njesuthi at its confluence with Poacher's Stream. This crossing can be difficult or impossible especially in December in which case the alternative start using Walk 38 can be used. On the other side the path starts L but immediately bends back R to cross Poacher's Stream after 300m. Then it pushes uphill S in the direction of a large buttress which divides the valleys of Poacher's Stream and the Njesuthi river. From here you walk easily back down towards the river, initially separated from it by a small hill pt 1614m.

Eland are common here and we saw fresh leopard tracks in this area. At c4.4km note a small path going down R to the river (SP Marble Baths) and just 400m further on cross a small tributary of the Njesuthi before climbing up S to the razor-wired compound of Battle Cave, 500m distance from the stream crossing. (The path you have been following goes on to Lower Injisuthi cave.) ▷

The well-known landmark of the Yellowwood tree splitting the rock on the way to Battle Cave

Return the same way.

WALK 43
Marble Baths

Start	Injisuthi Camp
Distance	19km
Ascent	950m
Grade	Moderate
Time	7–8hrs

Follow Walk 40 to the main **Grindstone Cave**. Continue for 200m and find a SP. Turn up L here and go through the rocky

This is a great destination in its own right for relaxation, play or swimming. It can be reached more quickly as a 'there-and-back' trip via the Njesuthi valley (see Walk 42) or make the longer expedition, as described here, over the Little Berg.

band onto the Little Berg to reach a stone sign after 1km (c2020m). The map indicates a small path continuing W and then descending to cross Old Woman Stream but this was neither signposted nor evident at the time of writing. Indeed, the only visible path is the one you are following.

Follow it L (SW) but note that it is not in accord with the map. Actually it contours S around the high ground staying firmly between 2020m and 2040m, crossing a deep re-entrant at the same level. From here it heads SE to round the SE spur of the Gibisila ridge, still at 2040m, and is joined by the faint trace of the **Contour Path**. To this point the level and easy ground makes for quick progress.

Across the **spur** you go and the path loses height quickly down to the valley wherein lies a **tributary** of the Njesuthi which runs down from between Old Woman Grinding Corn and The Ape. Here you are at c1865m and, after crossing to the S bank, follow cairns to pick up the track that leads downstream, mostly easy to follow and always within 20m of the stream. Lower down you suddenly veer R over open grassland and through scrub to descend finally to the superb **Marble Baths** (c1790m).

This is a place of a narrow channel, in some places quite deep, in others just a bum slide, where water has eroded the rock. ◄

To continue, cross the river (cairns) and climb steeply up to where **Marble Baths Cave** lies just above. The path contours at c1800m for over 1km, gradually turning E, and then begins its descent to the river at two rocky knolls on your L. Finally it crosses the **Njesuthi** to get up onto the **Battle Cave path** (Walk 42). This crossing and the way up to the path is indistinct so you may have to fight your way up the few metres to reach the path home.

In sunshine it is a particularly spectacular place which invites a leisurely stop.

GIANT'S CASTLE (1750M)

Giant's Castle camp with the impressive Giant's Castle peak

Giant's Castle epitomises the Maloti-Drakensberg Park. Steep-sided valleys radiate out from the beautifully sited and very comfortable large camp giving good access routes to the Little Berg. The backdrop of the basalt cliffs of the escarpment, dominated by Giant's Castle peak itself, completes the picture. Even the approach along the Bushman's River, mountain walls gradually closing around you, heightens the atmosphere.

GETTING THERE

From OR Tambo International Airport, Johannesburg
Follow the N3 (SP Durban) to exit 175, c410km from the airport. At the top of the slip road turn R (W). The road is surfaced and signposted to Giant's Castle all the way (58km) with only two significant road junctions towards the end of the route.

From King Shaka International Airport, Durban
Leave the airport via the connection to the N2, the main N–S coastal route. Drive S for about 30km to the interchange with the N3 (SP Pietermaritzburg). Once established on the N3 heading N continue as far as exit 132 for Nottingham Road and drive 8km to that small town (supermarket, cafés, all good for self-caterers). Then follow signs for R103 SP Rosetta 8km further on, although blink and you'll miss it. Turn L (SP Kamberg Camp & Rock Art Centre), later passing turnings for Kamberg and Highmoor and continuing on the same road all the way to Giant's Castle (60km from Rosetta).

FACILITIES

Mooi River has an ATM, post office, pharmacy, supermarket and petrol.

There is no accommodation outside and close to the Park. This means a lengthy drive from other establishments along the roads leading in from the N3 axis. This is important as Giant's Castle camp is often heavily booked. Antbear Guest House (www.antbear.co.za) can be recommended but is some distance away.

At Park HQ there is an excellent hutted camp and a campsite. Only minimal supplies are available here but there is a restaurant. A mobile phone signal may be elusive in the camp and is best near reception.

MAP REQUIRED

KZN Wildlife uKhahlamba-Drakensberg Park Hiking Map 3

WALK 44

Main Caves and River Walk

Start	Camp reception
Distance	5km
Ascent	175m
Grade	Easy
Time	1hr 30mins

This may not be the top site for cave art in the Drakensberg but it is a good show and a short walk. The river walk back is very beautiful and there are a number of terrific spots for a waterside picnic. You must purchase a ticket in advance from the camp office for the guided tour.

Opposite the camp reception a signpost directs you to the Main Caves. The concrete path runs S out past some chalets onto open hillside with lovely views ahead up towards Giant's Castle itself. After a little more than 1km, fork L at a SP, the R fork alternative heading off towards the major walks to the W. Just ahead is a lovely

The re-creation of Bushman life at Main Caves

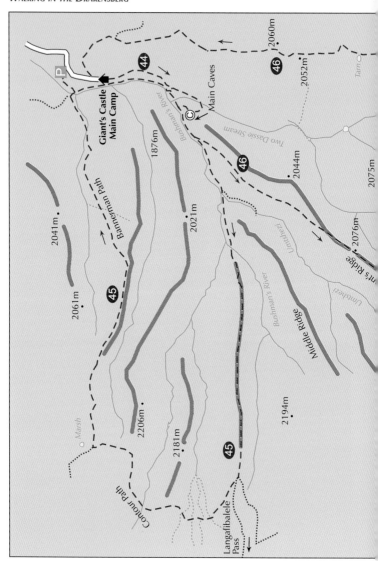

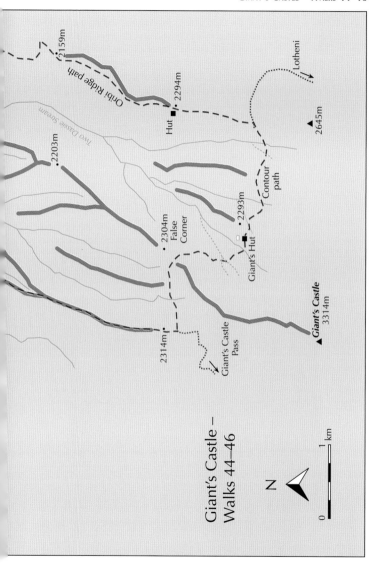

Giant's Castle –
Walks 44–46

N

0   1 km

spot. The path crosses **Two Dassie Stream**, a perfect resting point even though the way has been easy. Next, go up steps quite steeply to where you turn back on yourself through woodland and past Dassie Rock. Ignore the sandstone mess and apparent paths on the cliffs to your L and go straight on just 50m or so, descending slightly, to the gate and fence where the guide for the **caves** will meet you.

There are two options for the return walk. Both start on the N side of the cliff where the tour takes in more caves and paintings. The nicest way is to descend to the junction where a path goes L for the higher mountains: turn R here and go down over the small stream and immediately turn L. This leads to the **Bushman's River** and a delightful riverside walk back towards Giant's Castle Camp. The preferred route keeps L and follows the river rather than making the ascent directly to the camp buildings. It emerges eventually at the **Bannerman Bridge** where a R turn takes you up exceeding steeply to the picnic site and day-visitor **car park**. ◀

Don't forget to take in historic Rock 75 if you haven't already seen it (see Walk 45).

WALK 45

Langalibalele and Bannerman Ridges

Start	Camp reception
Distance	17km
Ascent	825m
Grade	Moderate
Time	5hrs 30min

A big ridge-walk start with a continuation via the contour path and an easy grassland descent. Can be quite lonely, but no route-finding problems and no exposure.

ROCK 75

This is a large boulder with the number 75 chiselled into it, effected by the  regimental cook of the 75th Regiment of Foot (from 1881 The Gordon Highlanders), some of whom were at that time under the command of Colonel Durnford (Royal Engineers). In 1874 he was tasked with blowing up all the passes between the then Natal Colony and present day Lesotho to stop border incursions by stock rustlers and other miscreants. Interestingly, today the same issue of illegal border crossing pertains with stock rustling and 'dagga' (marijuana) smuggling and occasional shoot-outs with police or Park Rangers.

Follow Walk 44 as far as the first SP and there go down R. Just 300m down the hill you reach the bridge over **Two Dassie Stream**. Just before the crossing consider making a small diversion R to 'Rock 75'.

LANGALIBALELE PASS

Ahead lies Langalibalele Pass, a significant landmark in British military history. Here, in 1873, the then Major Durnford (RE), in attempting to defeat the Hlubi chief Langalibalele, got into all sorts of organisational, navigational, administrative and disciplinary difficulties. Three troopers of the Natal Carbineers, a Basotho scout and Elijah Kambule, the interpreter, were killed. Their grave is up at the pass, over 700m up from where you are, but with no difficulties en route. Note that the peaks around bear the names of the fallen.

To continue, cross Two Dassie Stream and 400m further on fork R along the **Bushman's River** (L is for Giant's Ridge: see Walk 46) and continue for 1km to a

Langalibalele Ridge from the confluence of Bushman's River and Umtshezi stream

SP at another fork just at the **confluence** of Umtshezi and Bushman's rivers. Go down R to cross the **Umtshezi** stream (L is Grysbok Bush) and about 800m further on, cross what is probably **Bushman's River**. At this point the path takes off steeply. Go up the spur which comes down from Langalibalele Ridge but then avoid a high point before hitting the **ridge crest** at c2010m. The steepest section is now over. There is one knoll ahead with erosion barrier 'steps' (c2110m) and then largely easy ground all the way up the ridge to the crossroads with the **Contour Path** (c2256m).

Turn R at the crossroads. The Contour Path does what it says and is easy to follow. After 3.6km you arrive at another signpost where the Bannerman Hut lies ahead and you turn R (E). It is 5.5km from here down to the Bushman's River below the camp over easy grassland. After first crossing the small **stream** that has accompanied you down the final valley, continue 200m to cross the **Bushman's River** by a bridge and soon turn L at a signpost (straight on is the riverbank walk). This largely concreted, steep path brings you out after one hairpin bend at the visitors' **car park**. Turn R and walk down the road back to the main camp.

160

WALK 46

*Giant's Hut: up via Giant's Ridge and
down via Oribi Ridge*

Start	Camp reception
Distance	22km
Ascent	900m
Grade	Strenuous
Time	7–8hrs

This is the best day walk in the area, but a tough and genuine ridge walk. Ascending Giant's Ridge you have Giant's Castle in your face all the way. The hut was ruined by lightning strike in 2007 and partially rebuilt in 2015. Having expended prodigious volunteer energy, emotional, physical and financial, an unusually high wind blew off the partially completed roof. In June 2016 it was still unusable.

Use the route for Walk 45 as far as the fork 400m after the **Two Dassie Stream** crossing. The path goes up L quite steeply through the sandstone cliffs but soon settles down to gain height gradually up the W side of the spur of **Giant's Ridge**. You reach the ridge proper at c2015m and then just follow the crest. At some rocks (c2155m) the path dives L into a small re-entrant but soon emerges on the crest again. A modest cairn (c2325m) heralds the final flat 600m section to the junction with the **Contour Path** (c2340m). No SP at the time of writing, but turn L (E) and follow easily around **False Corner**, finally crossing two small streams before arriving at **Giant's Hut** with its tarn close by. In the dry season this is an unimpressive water feature but much more scenic in summer. ▸

Eland, Blesbok and Grey Rhebok were in the vicinity at the time of our visit.

 Leave the hut E and cross the rocky stream, climbing a little on the other side. The path junction to turn N for Oribi Ridge is very unclear and there was no SP in 2009, but essentially aim for the obvious cairn which marks **pt2294m**. In mist this will be tricky and demand care or a reversal of route. Just the other side of and below this point is a small

The path up Giant's Ridge with Giant's Castle Pass ahead

hut marked on the map as 'ruined'. In fact it has a roof and would be a reasonable shelter in adverse weather.

Two Dassie Stream lies below you on the L as you begin a sharp descent. The path rarely follows the ridge crest. There is a loss of height to a broad col at c2100m and after regaining some height and staying E of the ridge find a **tarn** at c2110m. Then pass E of **pt2052m** and descend to another col at c2000m. Regain height again to pass W of **pt2060m**, the path subsequently taking the E side of the high ground. After a short but obvious steep zig-zag you arrive down on flattish moorland and meet the path from Meander Hut at c1860m. Keep straight on and 1km brings you down onto the camp access road close to reception.

WALK 47

*Over Beacon Ridge to the viewpoint with an
optional extension to Meander Hut*

Start	Camp reception
Distance	8km
Ascent	350m
Grade	Easy
Time	3hrs 30min

Highly enjoyable and not too steep shorter walk with great all-round views.
You can extend it if you wish to the currently ruined Meander Hut, roofless
and complete with rusting bed frames.

Walk back down the camp entrance road for 150m and
take the path up R (SP). Ignore a small path on the R
just after the start and also the paths on the L rising from
Ranger HQ. You go round a corner and enter a narrow

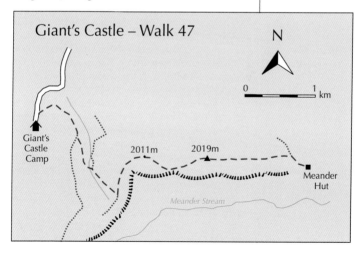

BEWARE OF CROW
WITH A RUBBER FETISH
PLEASE COVER
WINDSCREEN WIPERS.

PARKING FOR
OVERNIGHT HIKERS

NOTICE
TO VISIT THE MAIN

Health and safety warning in the visitor's car park at Giant's Castle

Here you look into the Meander valley.

valley with a stream down to the L. The valley soon opens out and brings you to a signposted fork 1km from the start. Keep L (R is for Oribi Ridge). You are now in a wide moorland basin and after 500m cross a tiny **stream** to go up to another fork and SP. Keep R (SP Meander Hut) and climb easily up the flank of the hill to the **crest** ahead. ◀ Turn L and head uphill to **pt2011m**. After a descent of some 40m go up the ridge again to the stone pillar marking the highest point (**2019m**). Return the same way.

To extend the walk to the **Meander hut** continue in the same line downhill and resolutely E. At the bottom of the hill, where the ground levels out, curve R on the far side of a re-entrant to find a small sign with a steep downhill path round a corner for 100m to the ruin. It is a place of great solitude and beautiful vistas. The cost of this extension is an extra 3.5km and over 150m climb.

Either retrace your steps or return to the small sign and head N (no path) for c350m to hit a management track. Turn L and follow it back to the road then L for the camp. At 6.5km this is longer but much easier.

HIGHMOOR (1980M)

The narrow path taking you in to Aasvoëlkrans Cave (Walk 49)

Highmoor is exactly what it says on the tin. It is very similar country to British moor-land and the routes involve tramping along relatively level ground rather than the steep stuff in other areas. Although it sits squarely around the 2000m mark the peaks of the escarpment are just that bit further away here when compared with the centres to the north. The 4km of surfaced road from entrance sign to car park goes up steeply along the Little Mooi stream between grassy hills and their sandstone outcrops; indeed it is one of the few places where you can drive onto the Little Berg.

GETTING THERE

From OR Tambo International Airport, Johannesburg
Follow the N3 (SP Durban) to exit 143, c443km from the airport. This is the more southern of the two Mooi river exits. Then use R103 S to the hamlet of Rosetta. Turn W here and drive to Glengarry where you turn L onto an unsurfaced road (signposted). It is about c40km to the Park from the N3. You reach tarmac again just inside the Park boundary for the last stretch to the administrative buildings, car park and campsite.

From King Shaka International Airport, Durban
Leave the airport via the connection to the N2, the main N–S coastal route. Drive S for about 30km to the interchange with the N3 (SP Pietermaritzburg). Once established on the N3 heading N, continue as far as exit 132 for Nottingham Road. From there follow signs for Rosetta and there turn L and follow as above.

FACILITIES

Mooi River has an ATM, post office, pharmacy, supermarket and petrol. Nottingham Road has the same facilities but a better supermarket and a nice choice of cafés.

There is limited accommodation within a short distance of the Park. Top of a very short list is the superb but rather pricey Cleopatra Mountain Farmhouse with its exquisite cuisine (www.cleomountain.com). At Park HQ there is a campsite but no accommodation and no shop.

MAP REQUIRED

KZN Wildlife uKhahlamba-Drakensberg Park Hiking Map 4

WALK 48
Foulton's Rock

Start	Highmoor car park
Distance	10.5km
Ascent	530m
Grade	Moderate
Time	4hrs

This walk has a straightforward beginning, but with steep ground and route-finding issues to finish, and takes you to a good little rock art site where you can see everything from outside the wire. If you want to go in you should take a guide rather than trying to squeeze past the stanchions.

Leave NW from the car park and turn R at the sign after the gate. After 250m cross the **stream** and another 250m on ignore the small path R (for Walk 49). On the R you see **Kamloops Dam** and the path crosses the inflow stream with the **Salma Dam** to the L. It is easy going. You

Coming down the spur with Foulton's Rock visible right of centre

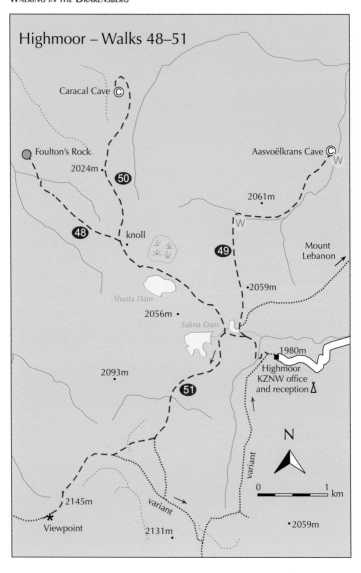

Highmoor – Walks 48–51

Caracal Cave Ⓒ

Foulton's Rock

2024m

50

Aasvoëlkrans Cave Ⓒ W

2061m

48

knoll

W

49

Mount Lebanon

2059m

Shasta Dam

2056m

Salma Dam

1980m

Highmoor KZNW office and reception

2093m

51

N

0   1 km

variant

2145m

variant

Viewpoint

2131m

2059m

then pass the **Shasta Dam** on your L, but it is easy to miss when distracted by the huge mass of the peak of Giant's Castle in the distance to the WSW. After passing a potentially **marshy area** R the path clearly veers round from its steady NW course to a more northerly one. At this point there is a small **knoll** on your R, and 200m along the path from there, a very small track leaves the main path and heads NW across a grassy spur.

About 250m along the spur the descent begins and it does so over a series of rocky steps. The path becomes extremely steep and then abruptly disappears. ▶

The photograph here may make navigation much easier. There is a small plateau before the final step down to the river below and your next waypoint is there, a **stream** course close at hand on the R. Make your way to this and look for a tiny wooden bridge. You cannot see your destination from there. Across the stream a more obvious path arises which takes you in about 600m to **Foulton's Rock** (c1720m). Return the same way.

Foulton's Rock can be seen for much of the descent if you know what to look for.

WALK 49
Aasvoëlkrans (Vulture) Cave

Start	Highmoor car park
Distance	8km
Ascent	220m
Grade	Easy
Time	3hrs

An open moorland walk past waterfalls to a good cave. The views extend to Monk's Cowl and, closer, the Drakensberg Wetlands Project.

Use the route for Walk 48 to start, but 250m after the **stream crossing** take the small path R which leads to the small **Kamloops Dam** wall. Cross this to a junction where you take the L fork. This leads gently uphill with **pt2059m** to your R. Over the skyline you ease downhill to cross the **stream** that runs W–E ahead of you. There is a small **waterfall** immediately downstream of this crossing.

Now the path turns E on the N bank of the stream and below the high ground (**pt2061m**). It stays above the river and later crosses a small spur and descends towards a viewpoint where the path ends. Just before this, steep steps lead down R and continue as a narrow and slightly exposed but short path, round to the R and into the **Aasvoëlkrans cave**, which is nicely situated some way above a waterfall. Return the same way.

WALK 50
Caracal Cave

Start	Highmoor car park
Distance	10km
Ascent	300m
Grade	Easy
Time	3hr 30mins

Another open moorland walk with superb panoramic views and a good chance of game sighting.

Follow the route for Walk 48 as far as the **knoll**. Go straight on where the path forks (L for Foulton's Rock). You seem to be following a spur, but soon it becomes apparent that this is not so and the ground falls away on the N side only to rise again a little further on. This is a good area to see game and in the autumns of 2008 and 2009 we saw families of Blesbok, Eland and Baboons here. ◄

In the distance to the NW the spike of Monk's Cowl and the flat-topped Cathkin Peak are visible.

The very small path goes steeply down from this high point and ahead on the L you will see two rectangular footings of old buildings. Keep going until you are E of these and note the deep re-entrant to your L. This is where **Caracal Cave** is. The path goes above and past the cave before turning down steeply into the re-entrant and leading back to it. History does not relate why the cave is named after a member of the cat family but there is usually evidence of recent human occupation by backpackers. Return the same way.

WALK 51
Giant's Castle viewpoint

Start	Highmoor car park
Distance	9.5km
Ascent	175m
Grade	Easy
Time	3hr

A walk on fairly level ground, easy to follow throughout. Blesbok and Eland are frequent sightings hereabouts and Cape Vultures commonly seen.

From the car park follow Walk 48 but take a left turn just before the outflow stream of the **Salma Dam**. Initially this leads generally SW turning more W at a fork. You go R and the path is identified by the wooden erosion bars. It is not plotted on the KZNW map at this point. After a small height gain it coasts around a re-entrant to your L and after passing the highest point of **c2145m** eases down to the viewpoint, the end of the walk. There is a man-made structure which at one time held an orientation plaque. The plaque has disappeared, but Giant's Castle is distinctive and looms high in the W.

Giant's Castle from the viewpoint

Either return by the same route, or take the alternative route back as outlined below (marked 'variant' on the map) but beware the inaccuracies of the KZNW map. The paths may be awkward to follow in poor visibility and anyone considering cross-country and possibly trackless adventures anywhere at Highmoor should have map and compass (or GPS) and the knowledge of how to use them. The advantage of this return route is that it takes you to the area W of **pt2059m** which is often rich in antelope. It adds 3.5km to the total.

Variant route: Retrace your steps to the point where the outward path begins to slip down L towards a small, sometimes dry, stream. Here, bear R on a trace of a track clearly used by vehicles in the past. At the time of writing, this junction was marked by a small cairn of stones but they may not be permanent! Walk SE for some 800m and meet the path from Salma Dam joining you from the N. Follow the now smaller path E for a further 600m, vague at times, until it swings S. You can either continue to pick up the northward leading path home a little further on or cut off the corner downhill – this is obvious. After a short dog-leg E, you resume a northerly heading all the way back to the Highmoor Office.

KAMBERG (1760M)

Bridge across the stream below Game Pass Shelter

This area is rather unlike the rest of the Park, being situated in a wide valley somewhat distant from the high Berg. The principal reason for its popularity is Game Pass Shelter, the renowned rock painting site, and the associated rock art Interpretative Centre. Fishing also is very popular here and the camp is often booked by fishing parties.

GETTING THERE

From OR Tambo International Airport, Johannesburg
Follow the N3 (SP Durban) to exit 143, c443km from the airport. This is the more southern of the two Mooi river exits. Then use R103 S to the hamlet of Rosetta. Turn W here and drive for c40km to the Park. There is a short unsurfaced section of road before you reach tarmac again just inside the Park boundary.

From King Shaka International Airport, Durban
Leave the airport via the connection to the N2, the main N–S coastal route. Drive S for about 30km to the interchange with the N3 (SP Pietermaritzburg). Once established on the N3 heading N continue as far as exit 132 for Nottingham Road. From there follow signs for Rosetta and there turn L and follow as above.

FACILITIES

Mooi River has an ATM, post office, pharmacy, supermarket and petrol. Nottingham Road has the same facilities but a nice choice of cafés and a better supermarket.

There is a hutted camp which is self-catering; it has no restaurant and only very basic supplies. Accommodation locally is sparse and visitors either stay in the camp chalets or drive in from the Highmoor area and further afield.

MAP REQUIRED

KZN Wildlife uKhahlamba-Drakensberg Park Hiking Map 4

WALK 52
Game Pass Shelter

Start	Interpretation Centre
Distance	7km
Ascent	280m
Grade	Easy
Time	3hrs

Game Pass Shelter is not just the top rock art site in the Drakensberg, it is also the end point of a pleasant and straightforward walk in itself. You are required to have a guide to get into the secured area and you should book in at the Interpretation Centre beforehand. The guide may already be up there.

Leave the **Interpretation Centre** (1760m) on the track leading S, and after 200m cross a stream before taking a small path L (SP). This is an easy section which, after

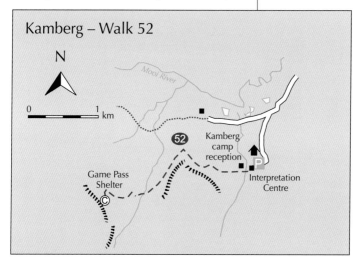

*Community guide at
Game Pass Shelter,
Kamberg*

steady progress W, rounds a **spur** to go S into a narrow valley. You pass behind a waterfall (seasonal) by a rock overhang and then cross the valley **stream** on a bridge (c1850m). A walk to here and a picnic at one of the pools upstream justifies the effort, even if you go no further. For the **shelter**, continue up steps onto open hillside where the path winds steeply up to the site gate. Return the same way.

LOTHENI (1470M)

Lotheni camp nestling below the high Berg

If Injisuthi is the hidden gem of the Drakensberg then Lotheni is the remote necklace. Certainly it is a longer drive on unmetalled roads than the other areas of the Park. However, it is well-worth the extra effort with its scenery, walking routes and, above all, tranquillity. The walking trails are well-signed and well-travelled but the connection to Giant's Castle via Taylor's Pass is vague in places. The much publicised Canyon Trail was 'closed' in 2009 and had been so for some time. Sheba's Breasts are neither particularly attractive nor worth the effort to conquer them but there is a respectable path to within touching distance.

GETTING THERE

From OR Tambo International Airport, Johannesburg
Follow the N3 (SP Durban) to exit 99, c487km from the airport. This is the southerly of the two Howick exits. Then take R617 past Boston and Bulwer as far as Underberg (115km). Turn N in Underberg (SP Himeville) and continue N through Himeville as far as Lower Lotheni which is signposted (c36km). After the Sani Pass turn-off the road is unsurfaced. At Lower Lotheni turn L (SP) and after c14km reach the Park entrance from where a tarmac surface takes you to the Park HQ in c5km. The camp is in the same place. The alternative access from Nottingham Road is much shorter in distance but the road is very poor and makes for very slow and awkward driving unless you have a 4x4 or pick-up.

From King Shaka International Airport, Durban
Leave the airport via the connection to the N2, the main N–S coastal route. Drive S for about 30km to the interchange with the N3 (SP Pietermaritzburg). Once established on the N3 heading N continue as far as exit 99 for Howick and then continue as above.

Underberg has an ATM, post office, pharmacy, supermarket, petrol and good places to eat. Himeville has few facilities.

There is no accommodation close to the Park. Inside the Park there is an excellent, superbly sited hutted camp (bring your own food, no power sockets), some cottages for hire for larger groups and a particularly nicely sited campsite. A variety of antelope visit the hutted camp at night and in the early morning.

FACILITIES

Underberg has an ATM, post office, pharmacy, supermarket, petrol and good places to eat. Himeville has few facilities.

There is no accommodation close to the Park. Inside the Park there is an excellent, superbly sited hutted camp (bring your own food, no power sockets), some cottages for hire for larger groups and a particularly nicely sited campsite. A variety of antelope visit the hutted camp at night and in the early morning.

Some simple provisions and souvenirs can be purchased at the Park headquarters, co-located with the visitor centre.

MAP REQUIRED

KZN Wildlife uKhahlamba-Drakensberg Park Hiking Map 4

WALK 53
eMpophomeni Falls and Eagle Rock

Start	Camp reception
Distance	14km
Ascent	500m
Grade	Moderate
Time	5hrs

A circular route in fine scenery, also known as Eagle Trail, taking in a small waterfall and a minor top. A shorter version saves about 2.5km. Beware the confusion potential of the KZNW map, which doesn't plot the outward leg path accurately.

Start on the road N towards the campsite, crossing the **stream** by the bridge (R) if the ford is too deep. Go past the site entrance and up to a conifer stand just before

Symes Cottage – available for rent

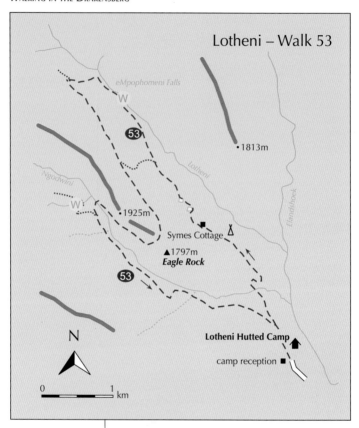

Lotheni – Walk 53

eMpophomeni Falls

W

53

•1813m

Lotheni

Ngodwini

W

•1925m

Flandshoek

Symes Cottage △

▲1797m
Eagle Rock

53

Lotheni Hutted Camp ⬆

camp reception ■

N

0   1
━━━━━━ km

Symes Cottage. A small signposted path breaks L and passes W of the cottage and its tarn. You climb steadily, passing a small **pond**, and up artificial steps to where the gradient eases. Here you are high above and some distance from the river.

At a fork a SP directs you down R towards eMpophomeni Falls. Straight ahead is the usual way to Yellowwood Cave and the shortened version of the Eagle Trail. The **falls** are c1.3km from this junction and the path goes right to the water's edge. The pool at the bottom is very difficult to access but it is a pleasant place.

Continue NW along the Lotheni on a less travelled but easy-to-follow path. After c500m it takes off steeply up L and gains almost 100m in height to a **T-junction** close to a wooded area and ruined building. The SP here is directionally confusing. Certainly to the R lies Yellowwood Cave but the vague path ahead leads nowhere. So turn L (SE) for the continuing Eagle Trail. This progresses easily across the hillside, just touching 1800m, and brings you to another path **junction**. To the L is the connection with the outward route (which also forms the short version of this walk) and R the Eagle Trail. You contour to a col at c1780m to pass between **pt1925** to the R and **Eagle Rock** to the L. You can easily shin up the latter for enhanced views of the Lotheni valley in a few minutes.

After an encouraging short descent directly towards the stream, the path disappoints by suddenly taking you uphill NW to a jumble of boulders and trees, before reaching the expected stream **crossing** where you turn for home. Just 100m after this note the small path R to another **waterfall** (only a small diversion) and, ultimately, the Contour Path. From this junction it is a straightforward descent of almost 4km back to the road close to camp reception.

Clear waymark on the Eagle Trail

WALK 54

Emadundwini Trail

Start	Camp reception
Distance	12km
Ascent	580m
Grade	Moderate
Time	4hrs 30min

A highly recommended circular walk through varied habitat including a large forest patch, protea-covered hillsides and a picnic spot to die for, all under towering sandstone cliffs. It is best done clockwise for an easier start and better views. For me, the star turn of Lotheni.

A compulsory picnic stop?

The SP opposite Reception directs you down to the Tebetebe bridge over the **Lotheni**. Cross the bridge, and a few metres up the opposite bank turn L at the SP. It is easy, level walking for more than 2km following first the **Lotheni** and then the **Elandshoek**, a major tributary. A small height gain precedes the crossing of a stream running down from the NE. This is where the work begins. Zig-zags lead up the W bank of this stream and then its W fork over a hillside covered with *Protea* trees, which are glorious in spring. At c1800m the path crosses the stream E and within 60m reaches a SP, the turn-off for Taylor's Pass and Giant's Castle.

Soon the path dives L into a thick **forest** patch, bliss on a hot

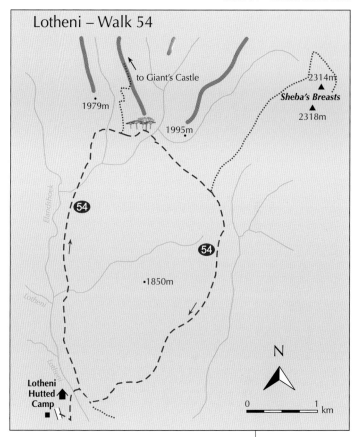

Lotheni – Walk 54

to Giant's Castle

1979m

1995m

2314m

Sheba's Breasts

2318m

54

54

•1850m

N

Lotheni
Hutted
Camp

0   1 km

day but don't dally there. Just ahead and out of the trees you go down to the river. ▸

Cross over and climb the other bank to reach the high point of the journey at around 1900m. Gradually the path turns SE and traverses open grassland to reach the signed **junction** for Sheba's Breasts, 1.7km from the picnic point. From here, over sometimes steep and rough ground, it is S and then SW back to the bridge and the start.

This is surely the luncheon and bathing spot of the area. It is a must-stop place.

183

WALK 55

Jacob's Ladder Falls

Start	Camp reception
Distance	5km
Ascent	190m
Grade	Easy
Time	3hrs

A very popular short walk to well-known waterfalls. They are scenic rather than spectacular but it is a charming, even dramatic, setting and well worth the short excursion. Seen in the right season, with the sun shining on the falls, the view is particularly rewarding.

Tebetebe Bridge over the Lotheni river

Follow Walk 54 to the Tebetebe bridge over the **Lotheni**. After crossing walk up a few metres to a SP. Go R (S)

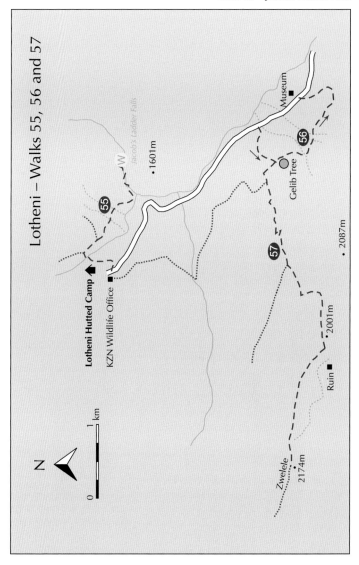

Lotheni – Walks 55, 56 and 57

N

0   1 km

Jacob's Ladder Falls

W

• 1601m

55

56

Museum

Gelib Tree

57

• 2087m

Lotheni Hutted Camp

KZN Wildlife Office

• 2001m

Ruin

Zwelele

• 2174m

and 200m further on come to another SP. To the L is the trail for Sheba's Breasts so go straight ahead. Cross two streams and then follow the path down to the bank of the Lotheni. This is just before the **confluence** of that river with Jacob's Stream which flows down through a narrow, steep-sided valley from the E. The path turns up this valley and crosses the stream seven times before you reach the deep swimming pool at the foot of the **falls**, just 600m or so from the confluence. Return the same way.

WALK 56
Gelib Tree

Start	Roadside SP 3.3km from camp towards the Reserve gate
Distance	2km or 5.5km
Ascent	100m or 175m
Grade	Easy
Time	40mins or 2hrs

A very short there-and-back stroll or a slightly longer excursion to a lone tree which has an interesting military history.

Leave the road at the SP. The path rises easily up through grassland for 800m to a SP. Just 100m ahead is the lone and shade-giving Acacia tree known as the **Gelib Tree** with its seat and memorial plaque, inside an enclosure.

To return either retrace your steps or, at the SP close to the tree, turn R. This path, marked at irregular intervals by stone signs with descending numbers, takes a circuitous route back to the road a few metres S of the Museum. This option has nothing particular to recommend it other than the creation of a round trip and further stretching of legs.

The Gelib Tree

THE GELIB TREE

In February 1941 South African forces were engaged in the invasion of Italian Somaliland. During this action, 11 Platoon of the 1st Royal Natal Carbineers were tasked with intercepting the enemy forces retreating northwards up the Juba River. Close to the town of Gelib (or Jelib) they were confronted by a group of Askaris with an Italian officer carrying a white flag of surrender. An officer (Lt DG Norton) and two other soldiers went forward to accept the surrender but, whilst negotiating, they and a section who had been advancing on the left came under heavy fire from enemy hidden on the flank and from the white flag party. Thirteen Carbineers were killed but miraculously Lt Norton survived.

Another regimental officer, Captain Charles Eustace, collected some seeds from an Acacia tree near the site of the action and, on returning home to his farm at Lotheni, planted them in memory of the fallen. Only a single tree survives today.

WALK 57
Zwelele

Start	Roadside SP 3.3km from camp towards the Reserve gate
Distance	12.8km
Ascent	750m
Grade	Moderate
Time	5hrs

A marked path and some trackless terrain take you up to an exceptional escarpment viewpoint without any practical difficulty and only moderate effort. The long ridge on which lies the proposed end-point of the walk is called Zwelele locally, but Ka-Zwelele on the KZNW map.

Looking NW up to the Escarpment from pt2174m

Use Walk 56 to the path **crossroads** just before the Gelib Tree. Turn R (SP) and go over fairly level ground for 250m, where you fork L (the R fork leads back to camp). For the next 2km there may be stretches of 10–20m

where the correct line is vague, but a group search for the wooden erosion/drainage poles brings swift results. Overall it is straightforward, the path winding up the hillside, steeply at times, onto a wide grassy shelf at c1800m. The next fork (SP) indicates L for Zwelele (R for the Canyon trail).

The hill pt2087m. An alternative top to visit

After a flattish grassland section you go steeply up through small rock bands, passing **pt2001m** on your L just before arrival at the col (SP) at c1990m.

From here, those who prefer a **shorter and lower** excursion could try the unnamed dome-shaped hill pt2087m, about 850m to the SE.

If you're up for the moderately more ambitious continuation to Zwelele, go WNW where traces of path are elusive. The best plan is to take the spur and its ensuing wide, grassy ridge direct. There are two steep sections before the final pull up to **pt2174m**, an unnamed top, which has outstanding views of a long segment of the escarpment. Return the same way. ▶

Of course you can continue along the ridge for as long as you wish until siren voices beckon you homeward.

COBHAM (1630M)

The Giant's Cup framed by Hodgson's Peaks (the S peak is on the L)

In some circles Cobham has a reputation for having little in the way of very large mountains. This is manifestly untrue. Hodgson's Peaks, acting as sentinels for Giant's Cup Pass, are each over 3250m for example. But the height is not 'in your face' as in Cathedral Peak. The first word that might occur as a description is 'beautiful' rather than 'grand' and it is a magnificent walking area with something for all. It is particularly good for sightings of Eland. One must also mention the frequent occurrence of Bushman rock paintings both here and in Garden Castle in addition to those more famous sites farther north in the Drakensberg.

The Giant's Cup Trail is a hiking route which, although some distance away from the High Berg, makes a fine walk either in its entirety or in stages. Conventionally hikers take five days to make this journey, from the start in the Sani Pass to the finish at Bushman's Nek, and make overnight stops at the strategically sited KZNW huts.

The Sani Pass is the only vehicle route from KwaZulu-Natal into the Mountain Kingdom of Lesotho. It is a spectacular and very difficult road which tops out at 2874m adjacent to both the Sani Mountain Lodge (meals and accommodation) and the Lesotho border post. The last section climbs 1330m in 8km. High clearance 4x4 vehicles are mandatory and even then it is a testing excursion and not for the faint-hearted. In winter it can be especially hazardous because of ice, and on occasion it is completely impassable because of snow. The South African border post is at the bottom. You require a passport for the journey over the Pass in both directions.

There are four start points for walks in this section. Apart from Cobham car park, routes also go from three points along the Sani Pass road – the Sani Pass Hotel, the Mkomazana Mountain Cottages and Sani Mountain Lodge (just over the border).

GETTING THERE

From OR Tambo International Airport, Johannesburg
Follow the N3 (SP Durban) to exit 99 c487km from the airport. Then take R617 past Boston and Bulwer as far as Underberg (110km). Turn N in Underberg (SP Himeville) and drive for c5km to the first few dwellings in Himeville village where there is a signposted turn L for Cobham. The Park HQ and campsite are 13km up this unsurfaced road.

From King Shaka International Airport, Durban
Leave the airport via the connection to the N2, the main N–S coastal route. Drive S for about 30km to the interchange with the N3 (SP Pietermaritzburg). Once established on the N3 heading N, drive as far as exit 99 for Howick and then continue as above.

For the Sani Pass Hotel drive N from Himeville for 2km and turn L at the crossroads (SP Sani Pass). The hotel is 11km from there on the R side of the road.

FACILITIES

Underberg has an ATM, post office, pharmacy, supermarket, fuel and dining options. Checkout the Lemon Tree coffee shop (wi-fi). Himeville has few facilities other than the historically well-known Himeville Arms but has many B&B establishments. Indeed, there is ample accommodation of all kinds in the most pleasant Underberg/Himeville/Sani Pass area. On the pass road consider the excellent value if rather basic Sani Lodge Backpacker's Hostel.

Inside the Park there is no shop and no formal rest camp. However, at the main entrance to the KZN Wildlife Cobham Office, apart from a campsite, there is the comfortable Pholela hut which caters primarily for walkers doing the Giant's Cup Trail, but if there is space casual visitors may use the facility.

MAP REQUIRED

KZN Wildlife uKhahlamba-Drakensberg Park Hiking Map 5

WALK 58
Trout Beck and return via By-pass Ridge

Start	Cobham car park
Distance	7.5km
Ascent	200m
Grade	Easy
Time	2hrs 30mins

An easy walk, outward mostly along a stream in a small valley with lots of places to stop, returning by the short-cut across the higher grassland. It starts by reversing the final section of day 1 of the Giant's Cup Trail.

From the car park walk back along the road and go through the campsite to cross the Pholela river by what the map calls a '**Swing Bridge**'. This seems somewhat perverse as there is a sign warning you not to swing on it. When you climb aboard you will see why.

Once safely established on the opposite, northern bank the path turns sharp L and after 1km parallel to the river you reach a stone SP close to the **confluence** of the Pholela and a tributary, Trout Beck. Take the L fork and after a few metres search for the cunningly concealed wooden bridge across the **beck** which will save you taking a false path straight ahead.

However, soon you encounter a different problem. There are just too many great places to stop and linger at the water's edge or indeed in the water.

From here on, the KZNW map is misleading as to the relationship of beck to path but it is easy to follow. ◀

Wind up the narrow valley of Trout Beck, the mass of Ndlovini ahead of you, to a final **crossing** after 3km where you go R and more steeply up the hillside to emerge on open grassland with scattered rocky outcrops. At c1800m there is a stone SP (for the Giant's Cup Trail) where you turn R (SE) to tramp gently downhill on a good path until there is a slightly steeper descent into a small re-entrant. Below this you go below a small rocky escarpment on your L to emerge at the **path junction** stone

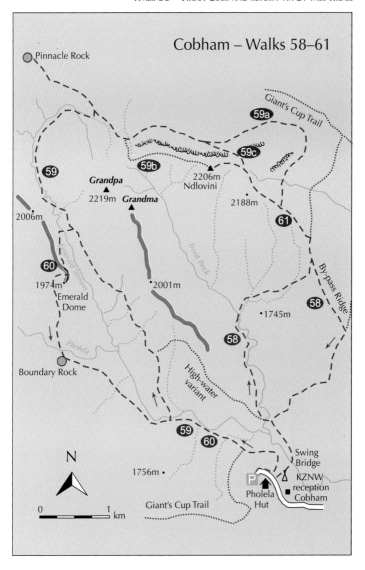

Cobham – Walks 58–61

Pinnacle Rock

Giant's Cup Trail

59a

59c

59b

59

Grandpa
2219m

Grandma

▲ 2206m
Ndlovini

2188m

2006m

61

Trout Beck

60

1974m

Emerald
Dome

2001m

Emerald Stream

Pholela

By-pass Ridge

58

•1745m

58

Boundary Rock

High-water
variant

59   **60**

N

1756m •

Swing
Bridge

P

Pholela
Hut

KZNW
reception
Cobham

Giant's Cup Trail

0   1 km

The old swing bridge – the new one also swings

NOTICE
* USE BRIDGE AT YOUR OWN RISK.
* DON'T SWING ON THE BRIDGE
* DON'T USE BRIDGE WHEN RIVER
  IN FLOOD.   *Thank you*

which completes your circle. Just 1km remains to take you back to the car park, doubtlessly swinging gaily over the bridge.

WALK 59
Pinnacle Rock

Start	Cobham car park
Distance	18km minimum
Ascent	400m
Grade	Moderate
Time	7hrs

A moderately long but straightforward walk with only modest height gain to an interesting group of rocks based around the large Pinnacle Rock. There are several variations for a round-trip.

Before starting assess the water level in the Pholela and if the level is high, use the variant start outlined below.

High water variant for Walks 59 and 60: (This is a 2km diversion.) Use Walk 58 to cross the swing bridge and follow it to the stone SP and across the 'concealed' bridge. After 20m an unsigned path breaks off L. Go L at the junction and continue, the path a bit vague at times through brambles and rocks after which it is easier to follow. You join the normal route soon after the path crosses a stream and turns SW, back in the valley of the Emerald Stream.

Otherwise, leave the car park N and follow the sign for 'Giant's Cup Trail second day'. Keep L close to the paddock fence and after c500m note the Giant's Cup Trail path turning up L. The path follows the river closely, at one stage going through a clump of oaks, and at 1.5km arrives at another stone SP. Branch R here to go down and cross

195

Pinnacle Rock on a brilliant September day

the **Pholela river**. This can be tricky, dangerous or obviously impossible at times of high water. After the crossing the path winds up through meadows, never too steeply, the **Emerald Stream** coming ever nearer on your L. You are aiming to pass to the L of the obvious *kopje* in front of you. ▶

Soon you go over a rise where there are boulders and trees for shade, and descend a little to the stream. **Cross** to the W bank and a little further on **back to the E**. You are now in a deep valley and the path curves round to the R along a tiny **tributary** of the Emerald Stream, the latter having come down from the NW. The colours around you confirm the origin of the stream's name. The valley is now much narrower and the path climbs up E onto a plateau as a prelude to switching back up NW to reach another plateau on which lies, rather obviously ahead of you, **Pinnacle Rock**. Although named after the tall spiky one there are a number of other large rocks at the same site which warrant exploration.

For the return journey retrace your steps for c1.25km of the plateau and then follow the path (unsigned) which contours round the N of **Grandpa** and **Ndlovini** (59a). This section is extremely exposed in places.

If you wish to detour to the summit of **Ndlovini** you have two options from this path. The **quicker ascent** (59b) is to turn up the slope to pass between the rocks of the Ndlovini W ridge (L) and Grandpa (R). At the col between the two find the easiest way up L onto the plateau of the summit ridge and walk E to the top. The **longer ascent** (59c) follows the contour path until it turns E, and then continues SE for about 1km. You will see a grassy col appearing as a gap between the tall sandstone buttresses N of Ndlovini summit. Pick your own route up to the top of the col. Once there turn R (W) and continue over easy ground, about 400m to the summit. There is a slight loss of height before the final few metres ascent. The highest point is at the N end of the final plateau. Return to the contour path to continue on the main route.

The contour path continues SE across the NE **ridge** of Ndlovini, east of the summit, before heading S, always close to the 2000m contour. Finally the route

As you go up the hill, note an area of forest reaching up towards the two hills called Grandma and Grandpa. This is often the haunt of Eland.

joins Walk 61 and, after a short and steep descent, emerges on the Giant's Cup Trail. Finish by following By-pass Ridge as on Walk 58 and on back down to the car park.

WALK 60
Emerald Dome

Start	Cobham car park
Distance	12km
Ascent	370m
Grade	Moderate
Time	4hrs 30mins

A respectably short walk with no technical difficulties to one of the best and easily-accessed viewpoints for the Giant's Cup.

Start by following Walk 59 as for Pinnacle Rock until you are walking up with **Emerald Stream** ever closer to you. Before you get to the obvious small *kopje* in front of you and when the stream is quite close look across to the hillside above the opposite bank. You will see a small path making a rising traverse towards the narrow rock band which marks the ridge that runs down from the NW to finish at Emerald Dome. Go down and **cross** the stream to reach the path. It takes you straight up to the base of the **Emerald Dome**. From there pick your own route up to the rounded grassy top.

To make an interesting round trip (provided the Pholela is crossable), reverse your route to the base of the dome and then turn down a grassy slope SW, subsequently following the W side of an obvious watercourse, aiming for Boundary Rock below you on the opposite bank of the Pholela. ◄

There are many pools which make a good place for a lunch stop.

Cross the river to Boundary Rock, then take the path which leads generally SE across open grassland, leaving the bank of the Pholela river for 1.5km but rejoining it where the path turns sharply L above lovely pools. Shortly after this you arrive at a SP where a path leads down L to cross the river (the outward leg of walks 59 and 60 go that way). Keep R, again leaving the river bank for a short distance, following the path through a small grove of trees including oak, to a large stone SP where the Giant's Cup Trail goes up R. Continue straight ahead, around the paddock, to emerge in the car park some 4.3km from Boundary Rock.

Emerald Dome with the Emerald Stream valley on the R

WALK 61

Ndlovini

Start	Cobham car park
Distance	14km
Ascent	600m
Grade	Moderate
Time	5hrs

A top walk with almost unlimited variations possible. A lot more is on offer than just ticking off another Drakensberg summit.

Use Walk 58, the lovely walk up Trout Beck, as far as the corner where that route turns R for home. Here go L and continue along the Giant's Cup Trail. After 200m the path goes through a clump of trees and you need hands to clamber through rocks at the end. After a further 100m you will see a small path rising up L. It is easy to follow, steep and takes a direct line right up to a col close to and directly E of the summit. En route you get increasingly close to a re-entrant on the R and at just above 2000m

Ndlovini seen from Trout Beck

note a small path joining from the N (see Walk 59). Some giant boulders forming the E flank of **pt2188m** herald the beginning of the end of the climbing. At the col turn W and go up the hill onto flat, stony ground with a slight descent before the final few m to the summit. This is about 400m from the col and is simply a pile of stones.

For the return or a continuation read the options for Pinnacle Rock, (Walk 59). You might wish to include this in your itinerary. ▶

This route also works well from Sani Lodge Backpackers or Sani Pass Hotel via Stromness Hill (see Walk 65).

WALK 62
Pholela River Walk to Boundary Rock

Start	Cobham car park
Distance	8km
Ascent	150m
Grade	Easy
Time	3hrs

A popular, fairly flat walk along the riverbank to a local feature. Ahead of you all the time is the Giant's Cup framed by the two Hodgson's Peaks (see Walk 68). Families often use this trail for picnics and swimming in the pool by the rock. Boundary Rock is considered to be the furthest point in the valley that an early explorer reached with wagons.

Follow Walk 59 for Pinnacle Rock for 1.5km and at the stone SP keep L (going R takes you down to the river crossing for Walks 59 and 60). Follow the river closely, rounding a bend R, before the path turns NW across grassland to cross a significant re-entrant. From here it is just 1.5km to the massive **Boundary Rock**, the end of the line for many.

You can explore the higher reaches of the Pholela without difficulty on a good path up all the way up to the valley junction at the Shelter (8.5km). ▶

A few hardy souls go all the way W to Lakes Cave to make a round trip, but this brings the day's total to around 28km with added height.

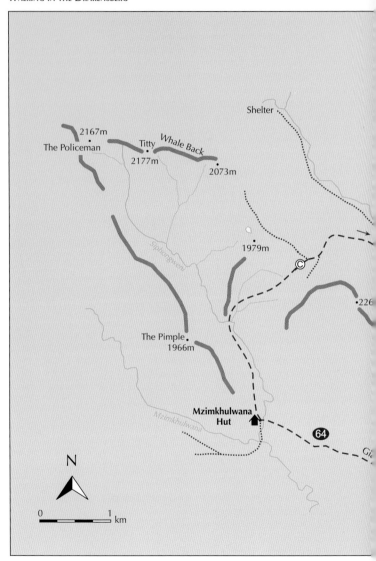

Cobham – Walks 62–64

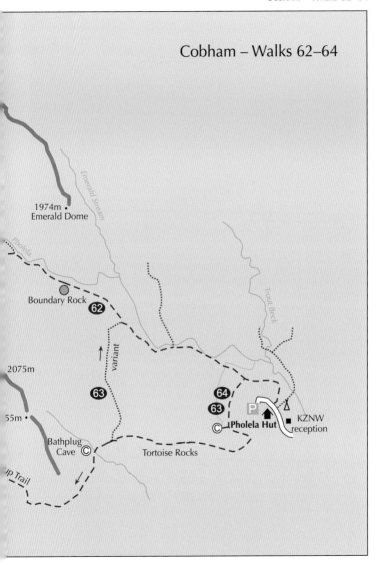

1974m • Emerald Dome

Emerald Stream

Pholela

Trout Beck

Boundary Rock

62

2075m

variant

63

55m •

Bathplug Cave ©

63

64

P

© Pholela Hut

Tortoise Rocks

■ KZNW reception

up Trail

The lovely Pholela River with Giant's Cup and Hodgson's Peaks in the distance

To return to the car park from Boundary Rock, follow the route for Walk 60.

WALK 63

Allen's Shelter and Tortoise Rocks

Start	Cobham car park
Distance	6km
Ascent	220m
Grade	Easy
Time	2hrs 30mins

An easy walk for even quite young children to a very interesting cave, nice rocks and a good viewpoint – and you can make it more challenging.

Follow signs for 'Giants Cup Trail second day'. This leads you N then W to get around the paddock and after 600m you bump into a stone SP where you turn L, still following the Giant's Cup Trail which, indeed, you follow all the way.

Go easily up the hillside to a small rocky escarpment. Here the path turns sharply back left (E). Look out for an unadvertised path close to this point going W into the corner of a small valley. This takes you to Allen's Shelter, a narrow cleft leading into a substantial **cave** where a small grinding stone remains as evidence of Bushman occupation.

Retrace your steps to the main path. This goes E, then more determinedly S, and finally W gaining height all the time, sometimes a little steeply but never awful. You pass the high point (c1850m) at about 2.5km from the start and from then on the trail runs just below **Tortoise rocks** which are above you to the left. The name relates directly to the unusual shape of the sandstone when seen close up. The best examples to linger by are at the point where they just touch the trail, at the end of the rocks. You can retrace your steps from here or follow the extension below for a somewhat longer, circular route.

Tortoise Rocks

For the more adventurous there is an **easy alternative return** over trackless ground. Continue along Giant's Cup Trail for just a few metres downhill until you pass a small group of boulders and trees on your R. You should see a small path swerving up rightwards which you follow onto a small plateau. Head a little W of N but don't gain height. When you go over a small crest you may find bits of path but essentially head N back to the path which runs on, or sometimes a little distance from, the S bank of the **Pholela** stream. The handrail which prevents you journeying too far W is the small stream valley running down from a rocky escarpment and from a source close to pt2155m on the KZNW map. Once you reach the Pholela valley main path it is just over 3km back to the car park.

This variation adds almost 6km to the route but with no significant extra ascent, and will take about 1hr 30mins longer. In poor visibility watch your compass but in mist this extension would be no fun anyway.

WALK 64

Mzimkulwana Hut,
Siphongweni Stream and Rock

Start	Cobham car park
Distance	19.5km
Ascent	750m
Grade	Moderate
Time	5–6hrs

A grand tour of the Cobham area taking in different habitats, a variety of views, some on good paths, some cross-country over rough and steep ground. There are interesting features all the way.

Follow Walk 63 past Allen's Shelter and **Tortoise Rocks** to where the extension of that route forks away R (N) at c1820m.

Now continue along the Giant's Cup Trail for another 700m until you wind into a small wooded area on your R. An obvious little path goes steeply up R into **Bathplug Cave**, so-named because the water entering from the ceiling goes down the 'plughole' beneath. It is an interesting place to explore.

Back on the trail there is a straightforward section heading SW towards the prominent Bamboo Mountain before the path swings W and gradually downhill to the **Mzimkulwana Hut**, refurbished in 2007. You have walked about 9.5km so far.

Take the path alongside the accommodation going N, a little way above the Siphongweni stream on your R. The valley is open here, the gradient easy and the way straightforward. Almost 2km on you must keep N up a small side valley, crossing the infant **Siphongweni** in one

Mzimkulwana Hut on the Giant's Cup Trail. Little Bamboo mountain is in the background

easy step. There is a just-about-detectable path to follow, going steeply up a grassy ramp to a prominent boulder and then following the little valley stream on its W side. All too soon a rocky outcrop bars the way. There is no path from here on up to the plateau. Cross the **stream** to the E bank and then head directly up very steep grass NE. When you surmount the first crest look ahead for a mushroom-shaped rock and walk steeply up to it (c1970m). Look out for the two well-known and characteristic summits to the NW, 'The Policeman' and 'Titty'.

The hard work is now over and you are on the edge of a fairly large plateau. Although the valley and its stream have also turned NE you have cut the corner. On the plateau to the NW you may see a small tarn (seasonally dry). Your next landmark is a pair of massive boulders in the same NE line of march. The grassland may be deep in this section but fortunately it is only c500m. Ahead lies the group of rocks amongst which is the huge Siphongweni Rock. ◄

Up to the R above you are the Easter Island-like figures with large foreheads that give Siphongweni mountain its name.

Around the back of the rock you will find the **cave,** which is large enough to sleep 12.

Walk out of the cave and directly ahead is a path and a **junction**. To turn L would take you generally along the E side of the plateau. Go straight ahead, still NE and level, to join a **path** coming from your R which has come down from the cliffs above. Now you start to lose height and the path drops into a gap in the rocky band marking the edge of the plateau. It follows a little stream for a while before crossing R onto a shoulder, then steeply and quickly down to the path in the **Pholela** valley.

You are now just 800m from **Boundary Rock** although the path depicted on the KZNW map suggests that it is well over 1km – this is incorrectly plotted. Follow Walk 60 homeward.

WALK 65

*Stromness Hill, Ngenwa Pool
and the Gxalingenwa River*

Start	Sani Pass Hotel
Distance	12.5km
Ascent	450m
Grade	Moderate
Time	5hrs

A varied and very scenic walk with the second half being the descent of the narrow Gxalingenwa valley, one of the best riverside walks in the Drakensberg.

GETTING TO THE SANI PASS HOTEL

Drive N from Himeville for 2km and turn L at the crossroads (SP Sani Pass). The Sani Pass Hotel is 11km from there on the R side of the road.

Over the road from the Sani Pass Hotel a grassy track leads straight up the hillside S. Higher up it veers L and follows a ridge directly and steeply up towards **pt1774m**, a kopje known as Stromness Hill. Just before reaching it you go through a gap in the fence to your R and contour, passing through another fence, to a cairn on the high point (c1768m) of what is a broad plateau. The panorama here is exceptional with the bulk of Ndlovini close to the W and, further away, the Giant's Cup. ▶

To the N are the unmistakeable Balancing Rocks and Nelson's Column and SE is Lifton Dam.

Turn R (W) and walk easily across the plateau losing only a little height. As you approach the small hill **pt1749m** note a path joining from the N – this is from the Sani Pass road. Keep W of the hill and then gain height up to the unmarked but obvious junction with the **Giant's Cup Trail**. Turn N. Soon the path swings NW and as it

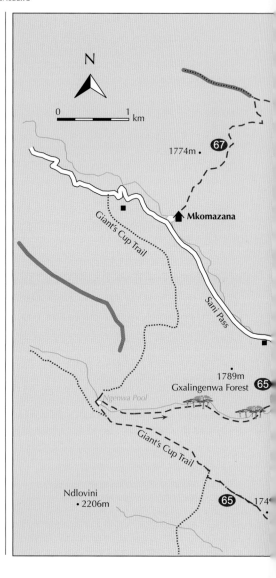

Cobham – Walks 65–67

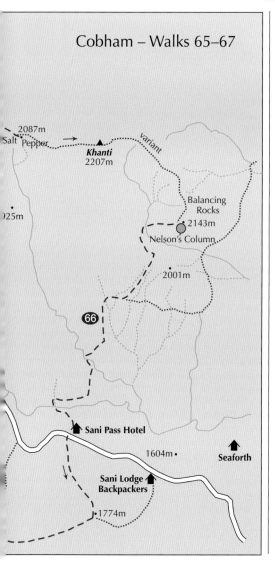

2087m
Salt Pepper →
Khanti
2207m

variant

925m

Balancing
Rocks
2143m
Nelson's Column

2001m

66

▲ **Sani Pass Hotel**

1604m •

▲ **Seaforth**

**Sani Lodge
Backpackers** ▲

• 1774m

Ngenwa Pool

descends you see way down R the deep, canyon-like valley of the Gxalingenwa. As the descent steepens you go down a protected rocky step into a cave with a waterfall. Just before reaching the valley floor note the small **path** heading NW and upstream.

Finally you get to the river at **Ngenwa Pool**, crossed by a stable log walkway. Even in winter it is deep enough for swimming if you can tolerate the temperature. Just up the opposite bank turn R at a fork (Giant's Cup Trail is L). You stay a little way above but parallel to the river until, after c500m, you go down to and **cross** to its S bank. ◄ Look out for the spot where the path, having gained a little height, suddenly dives back down riverside. There are obvious steps here. A false path ahead climbs up onto a rocky buttress and becomes increasingly precarious and vague.

From here on the path undulates and meanders close to the river, beautiful pools and cascades all the way, probably the best river walk in this book.

As you near the end of the downstream journey you cross the river three times and after a short section through woodland emerge on the Sani Pass road, about 1.5km from the start point. The hitherto dire road here is now an excellent surfaced highway. However, in 2016, it is still tricky to find the beginning of the route in the reverse direction.

Those who don't fancy the walk down the road often go through the gate to cross the hotel golf course but that cannot possibly be recommended by this guide.

WALK 66
Nelson's Column and Balancing Rocks

Start	Sani Pass Hotel
Distance	10km
Ascent	650m
Grade	Moderate
Time	5hrs 30mins

A steep but navigationally straightforward out-and-back to a top-notch viewpoint and most satisfactory rocky end-point.

Start at the Sani Pass Hotel. Go out of the back door, over the terrace and down to the golf course, aiming diagonally L (NW) to a swinging suspension bridge over the **stream**. ▶ Go up a very steep gully to the grassland at the top where the path goes sharply R. Gradually it turns N and then goes downhill to cross a small **stream**. From here resume the uphill march to a very small plateau at c1700m. Shortly after this go through a fence – you have now left the hotel grounds and have entered the Drakensberg Park and a notice reminds you of the importance of having an entry permit.

Now you are heading generally in the direction of a large sandstone buttress high above. The next important navigational beacon is your entrance into a small re-entrant where you cross a very small stream and then turn sharply R. Just before the stream there is a huge boulder on your R and, if you look up L, a strange rock formation

An entertaining crossing ensues: watch for those missing planks.

Nelson's Column

looking like a sombrero. I call this Sombrero Gulch. About 300m walking distance from here look out for the path junction (unsigned) where you turn L. At times of long grass this may not be very obvious.

The way from here on is not marked on the KZNW map. Soon the path becomes extremely steep and, higher up, was obviously made by someone who understood neither the meaning nor the helpfulness of zig-zags. After significant effort you reach another small plateau with, immediately ahead of you, Nelson's Column identified especially by his cockade hat. To the R and some distance behind Lord Nelson are the Balancing Rocks, less impressive from this angle.

A small path winds up and back L around a rocky buttress, several paces of exposure here, and brings you out onto a rocky area with cairns to guide you up a little and then down into a large grassy bowl. This avoids the embarrassment of cutting the corner and falling into a deep gorge with a stream. Go up the other side of the bowl close to a rock wall on your R, heading more or less E and, whenever you can, scramble up the large rocky area R and find the highest point. ▸

This should give you both a splendid look at the Balancing Rocks from their best angle and a great picnic spot. Two for the price of one.

WALK 67

Salt 'n Pepper

Start	Mkomazana Mountain Cottages Reception
Distance	8km
Ascent	375m
Grade	Easy
Time	3hrs 30mins

A short walk to an outstanding viewpoint, two 6m rocks standing side-by-side on the crest of a ridge. Neither condiment is easily scaleable.

Please read this important access note: this walk starts on private property. The managers of the property are often able and willing to give permission for a car to be parked for you to enjoy this walk. However, at busy times this may not be possible. It would be courteous to telephone beforehand to confirm arrangements (033-702-0340). On foot there is no problem.

As you face the reception office there is a small signed path on the grass to your L. After a short distance up steep grass the path goes through mixed woodland then more steeply again through a tree-covered rock band to a wooden SP where you bear R. Cross the slabby rocks (cairns) onto open grassland heading towards the ridge a little NW of Salt and Pepper. Shortly after crossing a deep and wooded re-entrant the path makes a dramatic dog-leg to the NW and arrives on the **ridge** at c1980m some 800m from the target of the walk. Pass a small perpetual

Walking up towards Salt 'n Pepper

Note that this area can be confusing topographically and only experienced navigators equipped with map and compass should do this, especially if there is a chance of poor visibility.

tarn on your L and you will see traces of path right up to the rocks. From here, return using the outward route.

The walk can be extended by going past **Salt** and **Pepper** on the N side and losing a little height before taking the obvious break in the sandstone cliffs to climb to the top of **Khanti** (or round it on the S). From there follow the fairly level ground in an arc trending S towards **Balancing Rocks** to return to the Sani road using Walk 66. ◀

WALK 68
Hodgson's Peaks (S 3256m: N 3251m)

Start	Sani Mountain Lodge
Distance	12km (S peak only)
Ascent	400m (S peak only)
Grade	Moderate (E at summit rocks of S peak)
Time	3hrs 30mins (S peak only)

This is one of the classic routes of the Drakensberg and very popular. It is quite short and with no real difficulties: there is very mild scrambling on the S peak. However, note the altitude and bear in mind its likely effect on performance. It can also be very cold and windy on the tops and appropriate gear is necessary.

Many local guides in Himeville/Underberg offer packages including driving you to Sani Mountain Lodge and taking you to the summit(s).

Remember to take your passport; you will be in Lesotho.

Leave Sani Mountain Lodge and pass the border post to turn SW on trackless terrain for about 1km, then go S to climb up to the small col at **pt3014m**. ▶

This is big, open and wild-feeling terrain.

On the other side of the col contour round to the SE on an old smuggler's path, soon joined from the L by a **path** from the col SE of pt 3115m. Note that this will be your return route.

Now track directly towards the base of the Giant's Cup, the lowest point between the two Hodgson's Peaks, known as **Masubasuba Pass**. There you will see the way

Lesotho shepherd traditionally clad in a blanket

217

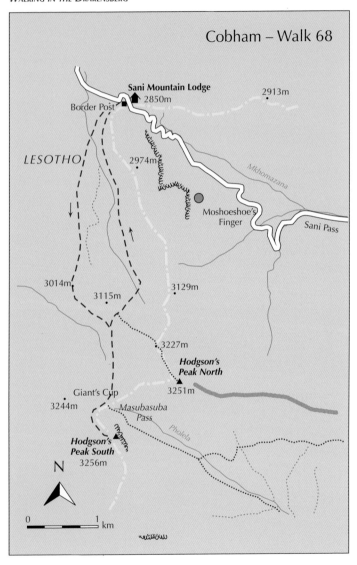

Cobham – Walk 68

Sani Mountain Lodge
2850m

Border Post

LESOTHO

2913m

2974m

Mkhomazana

Moshoeshoe's
Finger

Sani Pass

3014m

3115m

3129m

3227m

*Hodgson's
Peak North*

3251m

Giant's Cup

3244m

*Masubasuba
Pass*

Pholela

*Hodgson's
Peak South*

3256m

N

0   1 km

down to the Pholela Valley, which offers a possible but very long return walk to Cobham if you're anticipating a day-trip. Now climb up towards the rocky S peak passing through an obvious break in the small rocky band and then going up to the base of the **summit rocks**. Go round to the R (SE) and walk close to the rocks for c100m. There you will see signs of a small path which goes up in the same line (usually a cairn). Having gained some height on narrow ledges it zig-zags back L to gain more height and reaches a small chimney. Scramble up this on good holds. On the level ground above it is just a few metres to the obvious **highest point**.

To vary the return journey retrace your steps to go over the col SE of **pt3115m.** From here you can access the North Peak as outlined below, or to return to Sani Mountain Lodge go down to cross the small stream before heading down N to intersect with your outward route near the border post.

Hodgson's Peak North is much less interesting than its slightly larger namesake to the S. Walk to the col SE of **pt3115m** described above and then take the ridge to the summit direct, passing close to **pt3227m** on the way. You may find traces of path but essentially make your own route. The summit is at the far S end and has a couple of cairns. It adds 200m to your daily total if you do both peaks.

THOMAS HODGSON

In March 1862 Thomas Hodgson, a local farmer, was part of an armed group pursuing some Bushman cattle rustlers. Somewhere in this area he was fatally wounded by friendly fire. The story has it that he lies buried near the southern peak but recent research suggests that his grave may be some distance from here.

GARDEN CASTLE (1840M)

Rhino Peak seen from Lake Naverone

As you crest the final hill on the road to Garden Castle the panorama is very fine. It is rather reminiscent of Canada with a backdrop of high mountains and both deciduous and evergreen trees alongside a nice river. This is another gentle approach to the Drakensberg and another glimpse as to why the area is so popular for a multitude of activities.

GETTING THERE

From OR Tambo International Airport, Johannesburg
Follow the N3 (SP Durban) to exit 99, c487km from the airport, then take R617 past Boston and Bulwer as far as Underberg (110km). Continue on R617 for c4km and turn R at SP 'Drakensberg Gardens Resorts'. This hotel is 32km from Underberg. Go through the hotel boom and continue for 3.5km to the Park HQ and car park. Note that the final stretch of road to the office is unmarked on the KZNW map. Car parking is in a stand of Eucalyptus trees in front of and to the R of the KZNW Office and reception. Adjacent to the car park is a picnic area and the Hermit's Wood campsite.

From King Shaka International Airport, Durban
Leave the airport via the connection to the N2, the main N–S coastal route. Drive S for about 30km to the interchange with the N3 (SP Pietermaritzburg). Once established on the N3 heading N continue as far as exit 99 for Howick and then continue as above.

FACILITIES

Underberg has an ATM, post office, pharmacy, supermarket, petrol and good places to eat. There is a good store opposite Lake Naverone (www.lakenaverone.co.za), about 2km short of the hotel.

Apart from the Drakensberg Gardens Hotel there are self-catering establishments such as the excellent Naverone Lake, and some bed-and-breakfast accommodation on the road in from Underberg. There is ample accommodation of all kinds in the Underberg area but it is a long drive from there. Inside the Park there is just a campsite and a small shop in Park HQ which sells beer, soft drinks etc. Also there is the Swiman Giant's Cup Trail Hut which can be used, if not booked by Trail parties.

MAP REQUIRED

KZN Wildlife uKhahlamba-Drakensberg Park Hiking Map 6

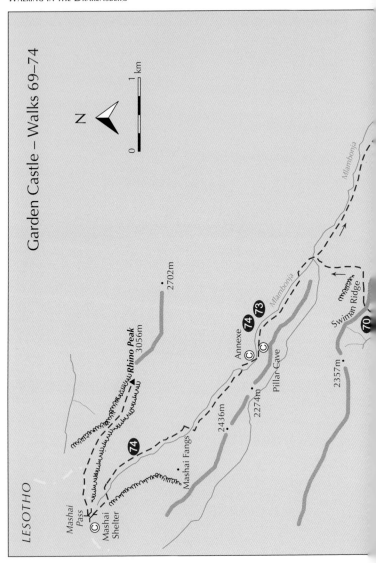

Garden Castle – Walks 69–74

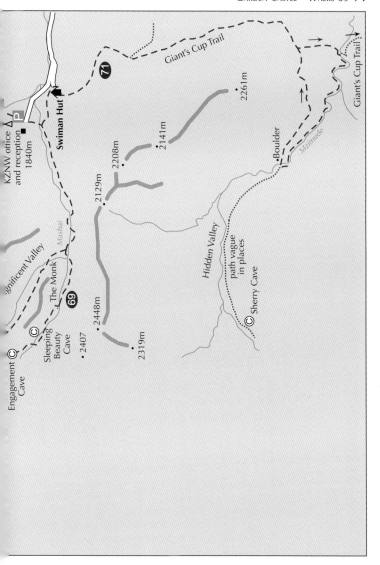

KZNW office
and reception
1840m

Swiman Hut

Giant's Cup Trail

71

2261m

2141m

2208m

Giant's Cup Trail

Boulder

Mzimude

2129m

Mashai

gnificent Valley

Hidden Valley

path vague
in places

The Monk

69

2448m

2407

Sherry Cave

2319m

Sleeping
Beauty
Cave

Engagement
Cave

WALK 69

Sleeping Beauty Cave and Engagement Cave

Start	Reserve car park
Distance	7km
Ascent	400m
Grade	Easy
Time	4hrs

This is a justifiably popular hike. It is not the cave that makes it so popular, it is the journey through astonishing sandstone cliff formations. There is a good path all the way. The final section to Engagement Cave is short and rewarding but requires a little route finding and minor scrambling.

I'm a bit of a Philistine about caves; they're useful for sleeping in, for sure, but 'seen one seen 'em all' is my attitude, although that's a little unfair on those in extraordinary locations or with stunning outlooks. The journey to reach these, on the other hand, really is worth the effort.

From the KZNW Office the trail is signposted S and leads gently downhill to cross the bridge over the **Mashai** river. Turn R (W). The path cruises easily just above the river which you follow all the way to the cave. The valley becomes wooded and narrows appreciably after c1.5km and after some 2km you cross the stream three times so you are then on the N bank. **The Monk**, hooded and crouching high above you, divides the Mashai valley from the valley locally-known as Magnificent Valley which now goes off to your R.

The fourth river crossing comes at the **confluence** of the Mashai and Magnificent Valley streams. At the fifth crossing you plunge into thick bush and things get much steeper, with a staircase to climb. All around are wondrously weathered sandstone formations. The last crossing is over the now baby Mashai and just above and to your

R is the massive overhang that is **Sleeping Beauty Cave** (c2200m).

It really is worthwhile making the extra effort required to reach Engagement Cave. Continue up the valley on a small path hugging the cliffs on the L. There are two awkward rock steps and a mild tussle with bamboo before you come to a boulder-strewn descent down R to cross the sometimes dry stream. A better path starts here and goes up steeply NE, soon emerging by a pyramidal-shaped rock in a flat, open and very pleasant valley. **Engagement Cave** is just 50m or so to the R and obvious. Return the same way. ▶

The brooding and hooded Monk sits between Sleeping Beauty and Magnificent Valleys

If you have time, some further exploration up here is rewarding.

WALK 70
Magnificent Valley and Swiman Ridge

Start	Reserve car park
Distance	10km
Ascent	650m
Grade	Moderate
Time	5hrs

A tough, and navigationally tricky challenge, through one of the most interesting geological sites of the district. The sandstone cliffs in Magnificent Valley (unnamed on the map) may be the most dramatic in the Drakensberg. This is a top-class outing introduced to me by the members of the Sani Hiking Club. Thank you guys, it was a great day.

Use Walk 69 to the third crossing of the **Mashai**, so that you are on the N bank. The narrow entrance to Magnificent Valley is on your R. A very faint path runs steeply up R and then becomes obvious as it zig-zags before turning into the valley proper, narrow and mildly exposed, quite high up on its E side just below rocky buttresses.

Further up the valley it descends to **cross** the valley stream and climbs again to the L of a very large boulder. Essentially you are following an Eland trail: the more frequently they have passed the easier to follow. You pass right up against a low black cliff, rubbing shoulders with the rock for several m.

Ahead and above L is a massive and sheer sandstone cliff and you progress past this to what looks like an inescapable situation as Magnificent Valley narrows dramatically. But a solution presents itself as the R-hand valley wall curves sharply R (N) and, alongside it, rising extremely steeply, you see a gully of grass and stones. **Cross the stream** and climb this.

Walking up into Magnificent Valley

Quite high up a rising diagonal path leaves L. You can use this but it is quicker to carry on up the very steep slope to where the gully opens out. Cross a minor stream bed to emerge on grass and rocky slabs just below 'Scottie-Dog Rock', a clearly shaped boulder ahead of you. Continue up, still steeply, past the rock and onto **Swiman Ridge** but not at its highest point.

A convenient lunch stop is with your back to this buttress, with the panorama towards Rhino Peak in front of you.

Walk about 150m SE through some rocks gaining only c15m height, then another 100m NE to reach the highest point of the walk (c2380m). On your R should be a large, yellow sandstone buttress. ◄

Ahead is one of the few straightforward ways down into the valley, descending over moderately steep grass and between rocky outcrops. Start just N of E and work your way down, gradually turning N and then NE. There is no path; choose the best line, descend with care, especially if the grass is wet, and change your route if things get awkward.

You should then emerge on the valley path along the Mlambonja stream, close to the **confluence,** with the small stream running down from the deep valley on your L. It is almost 3km from there to the car park on the excellent main valley path.

WALK 71

Hidden Valley

Start	Reserve car park
Distance	15.5km
Ascent	260m
Grade	Moderate
Time	5hrs

Start as for Walk 69 and cross the bridge over the Mashai river. Turn L (SP) and after 30m bear L again to avoid passing through the staff quarters. After 1km this path brings

This is a fascinating, go-where-you-like sort of walk. The conventional there-and-back route is available but there is also a variation described here, or create your own variations. Once off Giant's Cup Trail you rarely meet anyone, and once in the Hidden valley it feels very remote.

you to **Swiman Hut**, primarily for the use of those doing the Giant's Cup Trail, which starts behind the hut. The first section of today's route uses the Trail.

Just over 1km from the hut the path divides. Take the R fork which continues S over very easy grassland and slowly rises to a conglomeration of boulders at c1935m. This is an important landmark, for just 400m down the path, after it rounds a grassy ridge, is the almost imperceptible little path that leads to Hidden Valley (it was barely visible at the time of writing) which you will use on the return leg.

The large boulder in Hidden Valley where the path meets the river

For now, continue along the Trail, which dives down a narrow and rocky defile to emerge at a bridge over the Mzimude stream c1825m and 6km from your start point (5km from the Swiman Hut).

Stay on the N bank of the stream and follow a tiny path through the grass upstream. This is Hidden Valley. It really isn't much of a path at all and for the next 2km essentially you make your own way into the much wider area known as Hidden Valley. You pass through a narrow winding section, always close to the stream with excellent opportunities to sit, picnic, bathe, whatever. You will need to cross and re-cross the stream several times at spots of your choosing.

At the major **stream fork** take the R-hand, easterly option. Just over 2km upstream the valley broadens and you will see a gigantic boulder sitting in the stream with a nice pool on its E side. This is where the mapped path from the Giant's Cup trail comes down to the stream and is the suggested easy-to-follow way back. Upstream of the large boulder you can go as far as time and energy allow, exploring the main stream or one of the tributaries. ◄

It is a lovely, lonely place.

At times of higher water the crossings may leave you with wet feet. After a lot of rain in summer the narrow river valley may be unsafe. If that is likely take the traditional route on the map as a there-and-back walk.

WALK 72

Three Pools and Bushman Rock

Start	Reserve car park
Distance	8km (3 Pools only)
Ascent	300m
Grade	Easy
Time	4hrs

This is almost as popular as the Sleeping Beauty walk and a good children's walk, even though 60 per cent of the height gain is suffered on the return journey. The pools are deep enough to bathe in and it is good picnic place, well-shielded from any wind. A longer round-trip alternative is available by visiting Bushman's Rock.

You can make the journey easier by starting from Lake Naverone and driving down a rough road to a fence line but you need to seek permission from the folk at Lake Naverone.

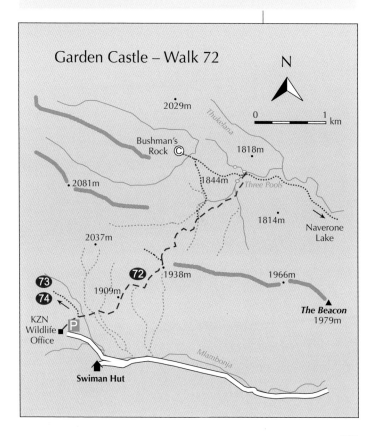

Leave the car park through the Eucalyptus stand called 'Hermit's Wood'. Fork R on the small path to leave the wood, cross the campsite track and walk over the grass to the stone SP. Turn R and take the **bridge** over the Mlambonja stream. The height gain starts immediately but is in two bursts separated by a fairly level section. As you crest the final **ridge** there is a splendid panorama of mountains and you can look down into the narrow valley wherein lie the Three Pools.

After a gentle start to the downhill section the gradient suddenly increases with the attendant nasty feeling about the return trip. It then winds down through grassland trending R. At c3km there is a small cairn and a rather vague path going L. Keep R and down into the narrowing valley where you walk along the bank of the stream, passing the **middle pool** and the **third pool** at a confluence. The first pool is behind you, 50m upstream of the middle one. ◄

Note also the excellent 'Champagne Pool' with its waterfall about 100m up the N-leading stream.

If you wish to visit Bushman's Rock, cross the stream from the middle pool to take a path which goes diagonally up the hillside and rounds **pt1814m** before setting

The middle of the Three Pools

off NW across the plateau. From time to time there are white footprint signs to guide you. Just before dropping down slightly to cross a stream you are joined at a small cairn by a path from the L. This is your return route. Cross the stream and go straight up for a short distance to the very interesting **Bushman's Rock**.

To return retrace your steps to cross the stream and then take the R fork at the cairn. This leads back to your original path from Garden Castle.

WALK 73

Pillar Cave and the Annexe

Start	Reserve car park
Distance	8.5km
Ascent	350m
Grade	Easy
Time	3hrs 30mins

Visiting Pillar Cave and the Annexe is a route that many quite young children can manage. Pillar Cave, so-called because of its central supporting pillar, is beautifully sited for views of the Clarens sandstone outcrops in a green cirque.

Leave the car park through the Eucalyptus stand called 'Hermit's Wood'. Fork R on the small path to leave the wood, cross the campsite track and walk over the grass to the stone SP. Turn left and follow the valley path along the Mlambonja, following the return route on the map for Walk 70. After almost 3km, at a **confluence** with a stream from your L, cross the Mlambonja to its N bank. At times of high water you may need to cross the small tributary first and then the main river.

After c500m cross back again. You stay on this S side now all the way to **Pillar Cave**, the path steepening just before arrival. ▶

It is a sunny place and has the benefit of morning sun too.

The supporting pillar which gives the cave its name

To visit the **Annexe** descend the path NW down to the river. Duck L at the large boulder and there find the correct river crossing. Just ahead of you up through the trees is the 2-bedroomed establishment, each offering at least a twin facility. Water is close, impromptu tree branch washing lines abundant but, sadly, no morning sun.

On the return walk consider turning L at the stone SP just before the finish line and adding 250m to your distance by visiting **Mermaid Pool**, a most delightful place to bathe feet and rest the body before going home.

WALK 74
Rhino Peak (3056m)

Start	Reserve car park
Distance	20km
Ascent	1500m
Grade	Strenuous
Time	9–10hrs

The silhouette of Rhino Peak when seen from the valley explains the name. This is a hard walk to a peak of dramatic appearance which, in the event, is technically simple. It is climbed frequently and worth every bit of the effort invested.

Walk to Pillar Cave and then the Annexe as in Walk 73.

To continue to Rhino Peak cross the river just below **the Annexe**. Then turn L and continue upstream to **re-cross** to the W bank at the point where the valley is at its narrowest, some 300m from the last crossing. The way is still clear here and the next **crossing** is almost 200m higher up at a U-shaped sloping sandstone slab on the W bank. In descent this is a particularly good landmark.

Most of the remainder of the climb up to Mashai Pass is E of the river, sometimes a way above it. The path can be tricky to follow but, particularly in descent, do not be lured into walking down/up the riverbed by promising-looking cairns placed there by the already lost. Up high on your L are the dramatic Mashai Fangs, tall rock pillars best seen from this angle.

Mermaid Pools with Rhino Peak in the background

As you get higher the path steepens considerably, continuing NW generally but ultimately curving almost W up to the pass. On this E side of the river there is much erosion and the best line changes year by year. At the time of our ascent it was best to cross back to the W slopes about 100m below the pass and traces of path are succeeded by a better path leading up to **Mashai Pass** (c2980m).

Mashai Fangs on your left as you climb up to Mashai Pass

Be prepared to vary this route depending on the state of the valley sides but, in descent, you will need to cross to the E bank relatively early and certainly before you have descended 200m. The ground becomes much more difficult lower down on the W side.

Note the tiny overhang called the **Mashai Shelter** just S of the path as it crests the pass, useful only in emergencies. From here it is very straightforward in good conditions, but beware poor visibility and high winds on the plateau on which you now find yourself. If in doubt turn back here.

The path, with some cairns, turns gradually SE on the almost flat and open ground of the plateau, rising only a little as it comes to the end of your just over 2km walk. On the way you pass large indentations, L and R, where the steep basalt cliffs have eroded into the plateau. Be very careful if the mist comes down.

The rocky bump at the SE end of the plateau is the top. It is a short and very easy ascent with mild exposure as you climb some boulders on the L side to reach the comfortable summit of **Rhino Peak** with its large pile of stones. Return the same way.

BUSHMAN'S NEK (1755M)

The higher of the Two Pools (Walk 75)

This is the southernmost outpost of the Maloti-Drakensberg Park and has a much more gentle feel to it than its more northerly colleagues. The scenery is still fine but the local mountains are undeniably smaller and less impressive. There is plenty of scope for easy walking and there are a number of caves with Bushman paintings for which local guides are compulsory and available. This is the end of the Giant's Cup Trail and the Bushman's Nek Hut, the final one of the journey, is nicely sited about 1km NW of the police frontier post close to the Trail.

GETTING THERE

From OR Tambo International Airport, Johannesburg
Follow the N3 (SP Durban) to exit 99, c487km from the airport, then take R617 past Boston and Bulwer as far as Underberg (110km). Continue on R617 (SP Kokstad) for c4km then turn R, signposted for Bushman's Nek. This road, all 32km of it, is still unsurfaced and can be in very poor condition.

From King Shaka International Airport, Durban
Leave the airport via the connection to the N2, the main N–S coastal route. Drive S for about 30km to the interchange with the N3 (SP Pietermaritzburg). Once established on the N3 heading N continue as far as exit 99 for Howick and then continue as above.

FACILITIES

Underberg is the hub for Cobham and Garden Castle with its ATM, post office, pharmacy, supermarket, fuel supplies and good places to eat. There is nothing at the Park HQ apart from a place to sign in and pay your fees. A small, basic map is provided.

There is a campsite and, inside the gate, the Bushman's Nek Giant's Cup Trail hut, which can be used if not booked by Trail parties but you must enquire in advance. The only hotel is the Bushman's Nek Berg and Trout Resort.

MAP REQUIRED

KZN Wildlife uKhahlamba-Drakensberg Park Hiking Map 6

WALK 75

Twin Pools

Start	KZNW Office
Distance	9km
Ascent	200m
Grade	Easy
Time	3hrs 30mins–4hrs

A straightforward walk to a delightful, clear swimming pool below a small waterfall in very grand surroundings. This is the start of an historic route into Lesotho over Bushman's Nek Pass, although nowadays it is very quiet except in school holidays. There is an abundance of lovely but smaller pools all along the way for those who prefer a shorter walk. A great opportunity to follow that great Drakensberg tradition of skinny-dipping.

Go through the border control post to where a SP directs you across the Bushman's river towards Twin Pools. Keep L where the path forks (badly signed in 2016), cross the Ngwangwane stream and walk on level ground up the broad valley. Ahead there is a lone Protea tree where the path is at its highest level above the stream (just over 2km of walking). Below are many splendid spots for playtime in the water.

Although the path divides just after this, either option suffices. The easier R-hand path goes down to cross the river and, after 200m, regains the S bank. As you pass the entrance to a valley falling down from the NW you get the first sighting of the spectacular Devil's Knuckles. The path then veers L to cross a small tributary of the main river and divides on the opposite bank. The L fork leads to Bushman's Nek Pass. Go right and after a little over 500m, staying on the path, you arrive at the upper and better of the 'Two Pools'. It lies at the point where a deep gully presents itself before you. There are many alternative possibilities if it's busy, but out of season you will probably have sole use.

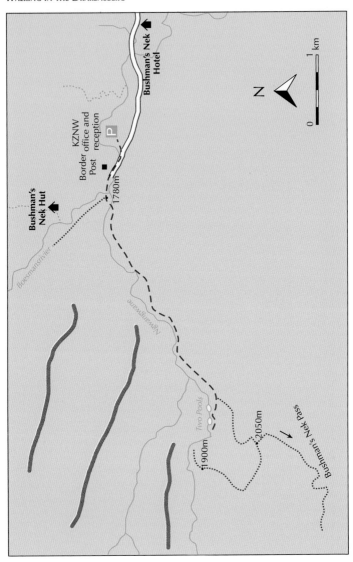

APPENDIX A

Walk summary table

No	Name	Difficulty	Distance (km)	Ascent (m)	Time (km)
Royal Natal National Park					
1	The Cascades	Easy	3	negligible	1hr
2	Fairy Glen	Easy	1	negligible	45min
3	Plowman's Kop Loop	Moderate	10.5	450	4hrs
4	The Crack & The Mudslide	Moderate/Strenuous	10	550/750	5–6hrs
5	Gudu Bush and Gudu Falls	Moderate	9.5	500	4hrs
6	Witsieshoek via Mahai Falls	Moderate	9	850	5hrs30min
7	Thukela Gorge Walk (to the picnic spot)	Easy	13	400	5 hrs
8	Policeman's Helmet	Moderate	13	475	4hrs 30mins
9	Camel's Hump (returning via Sunday Falls)	Moderate	15	650	5hrs
10	Sunday Falls	Easy	7	150	2hrs 30mins
11	Surprise Ridge and Cannibal Cave	Moderate	19	500	6hrs
13	Sugar Loaf	Moderate	7	600	3hrs 30mins

WALKING IN THE DRAKENSBERG

No	Name	Difficulty	Distance (km)	Ascent (m)	Time (km)
Cathedral Peak					
14	Doreen Falls	Easy	4	75	1hr 30mins
15	Mushroom Rock	Easy	5	400	3hrs
16	Rainbow Gorge	Moderate	15	350	6hrs
17	Ribbon Falls	Easy	7	350	3hrs
18	Xeni Cave	Moderate	11	550	6hrs
19	Tarn Hill Circuit	Moderate	8	650	4hrs
20	Tryme Hill and the Contour Path	Moderate	18	900	5hrs 30mins
21	Organ Pipes Pass and Cleft Peak	Strenuous	22	1900	10hrs
22	Baboon Rock	Moderate	9	550	4hrs
23	One Tree Hill	Moderate	8	500	3hrs 30mins
24	One Tree Hill and Contour Path into the Mlambonja valley	Strenuous	21	900	8hrs
25	Cathedral Peak	Strenuous	19	1600	10hrs
Monk's Cowl					
26	Nandi's Falls	Easy	8	250	2hrs 30mins
27	Hlathikulu Forest	Easy	9	400	3hrs 30mins

No	Name	Difficulty	Distance (km)	Ascent (m)	Time (km)
28	Crystal Falls, the Spinx and Verkykerskop	Easy	7	520	3hrs
29	Blind Man's Corner and Keartlands Pass	Moderate	12.5	700	4hrs
30	Matterhorn	Moderate	5	450	2hrs 30mins
31	Amphletts'	Strenuous	18	1200	7hrs 30mins
32	Sterkhorn	Strenuous	17	1550	7hrs
33	Injisuthi to Monk's Cowl	Strenuous	21	750	6hrs 30mins
34	Intunja/Gatberg	Strenuous	26	1400	9hrs 30mins
35	Blue Grotto	Easy	6.5	320	2hrs 30mins
36	Van Damm's Cascades	Moderate	12	550	4hrs 30mins
37	uMkhulumane Stream and Hlathikulu	Strenuous	21	850	8hrs
Injisuthi					
38	Poacher's Stream	Easy	4.5	200	1hrs 30mins
39	Van Heyningen's Pass	Easy	8	350	3hrs
40	Grindstone Caves	Easy	7	400	3hrs
41	Cataract Valley	Moderate	12.5	600	5hrs 30mins

No	Name	Difficulty	Distance (km)	Ascent (m)	Time (km)
42	Battle Cave	Moderate	10	425	4hrs
43	Marble Baths	Moderate	19	950	7hrs 30mins
Giant's Castle					
44	Main Caves and River Walk	Easy	5	175	1hr 30mins
45	Langalibalele and Bannerman Ridges	Moderate	17	825	5hrs 30mins
46	Giant's Ridge and Oribi Ridge	Strenuous	22	900	7hrs 30mins
47	Viewpoint with optional extension to Meander Hut	Easy	8	350	3hrs 30mins
Highmoor					
48	Foulton's Rock	Moderate	10.5	530	4hrs
49	Aasvoëlkrans Cave	Easy	8	220	3hrs
50	Caracal Cave	Easy	10	300	3hrs 30mins
51	Giant's Castle Viewpoint	Easy	9.5	175	3hrs
Kamberg					
52	Game Pass Shelter	Easy	7	280	3hrs

No	Name	Difficulty	Distance (km)	Ascent (m)	Time (km)
Lotheni					
53	eMpophomeni Falls and Eagle Rock	Moderate	14	500	5hrs
54	Emadundwini Trail	Moderate	12	580	4hrs 30mins
55	Jacob's Ladder Falls	Easy	5	190	3hrs
56	Gelib Tree	Easy	2	100	0-40
57	Zwelele	Moderate	12.8	750	5hrs
Cobham					
58	Trout Beck and By-pass Ridge	Easy	7.5	200	2hrs 30mins
59	Pinnacle Rock	Moderate	18	400	7hrs
60	Emerald Dome	Moderate	12	370	4hrs 30mins
61	Ndlovini	Moderate	14	600	5hrs
62	Pholela River Walk to Boundary Rock	Easy	8	150	3hrs
63	Allen's Shelter and Tortoise Rocks	Easy	6	220	2hrs 30mins
64	Mzimkulwana Hut, Siphongweni Stream and Rock	Moderate	19.5	750	5hrs 30mins
65	Stromness Hill, Ngenwa Pool and the Gxalingenwa River	Moderate	12.5	450	5hrs

No	Name	Difficulty	Distance (km)	Ascent (m)	Time (km)
66	Nelson's Column and Balancing Rocks	Moderate	10	650	5hrs 30mins
67	Salt 'n Pepper	Easy	8	375	3hrs 30mins
68	Hodgson's Peaks	Moderate	12	400	3hrs 30mins
Garden Castle					
69	Sleeping Beauty Cave	Easy	7	400	4hrs
70	Magnificent Valley and Swiman Ridge	Moderate	10	650	5hrs
71	Hidden Valley	Moderate	15.5	260	5hrs
72	Three Pools and Bushman Rock	Easy	8	300	4hrs
73	Pillar Cave and the Annexe	Easy	8.5	350	3hrs 30mins
74	Rhino Peak	Strenuous	20	1500	10hrs
Bushman's Nek					
75	Twin Pools	Easy	9	200	3hrs 30mins–4hrs

APPENDIX B

Facilities within the Park areas

	Office Altitude (m)	Accommodation	Restaurant facilities	Camp site(s)	Food & drink availability	Cellphone reception at base
RNNP	1400	Hutted camp	No	2	Minimal basic foods	Yes
Cathedral Peak	1480	Hutted camp Hotel	Restaurant Restaurant	1	Minimal basic foods	Yes
Monk's Cowl	1480	Nil	Small café	1	Nil	Yes
Injisuthi	1470	Hutted camp	No	1	Minimal basic foods	No
Giant's Castle	1750	Hutted camp	Restaurant	1	Minimal basic foods	Patchy
Highmoor	1980	Nil	No	1	Nil	Yes
Kamberg	1760	Hutted camp	No	0	Minimal basic foods	Yes
Lotheni	1470	Hutted camp	No	1	Minimal basic foods	Patchy
Cobham	1630	Pholela Giant's Trail Hut	No	1	Minimal basic foods	Patchy
Garden Castle	1840	Swiman Giant's Trail Hut	No	1	Minimal basic foods	Yes
Bushman's Nek	1755	Bushman's Nek Giant's Trail Hut	No	1	Nil	Yes

APPENDIX C
Useful contacts

The international dialing code for South Africa is 0027. If dialing from outside the country use 0027 and then exclude the first 0 of the internal telephone number.

KZN Wildlife
www.kznwildlife.com
For enquiries and reservations about hutted camps and camping within the Park at Royal Natal National Park, Cathedral Peak, Monk's Cowl, Injisuthi, Giant's Castle, Highmoor, Kamberg, Lotheni, Cobham, Garden Casle and Bushman's Nek, and also for enquiries about the Giant's Cup Trail Hut availability, email bookings@kznwildlife.com, tel 033 845 1000. (You can also download the current tariffs from the website.)

Daily rates per person for camping range currently from R60 upwards depending on site and facilities. Reservations are important. The KZN Wildlife hutted camps at Thendele (RNNP), Didima (Cathedral Peak), Injisuthi, Giant's Castle, Kamberg and Lotheni must also be booked beforehand unless you are extremely lucky on an out-of-high season day. The costs vary depending on the camp and its facilities and the number of beds in the hut/chalet. In 2016 a twin-bedded chalet cost from R520 (Lotheni) to R1000 per night at Thendele. Giant's Castle costs from R1160 which includes breakfast.

Other useful websites for the Drakensberg
www.drakensbergtourism.com
www.southafrica-travel.net
www.sa-venues.com
www.wheretostay.co.za/kzn
www.drakensberg.org (for the S Drakensberg – they have a useful booklet)

Royal Natal National Park
The Cavern Resort Hotel, www.cavern.co.za, tel 036 438 6270
Montusi Mountain Lodge, www.montusi.co.za, tel 036 438 6243

Cathedral Peak
Cathedral Peak Hotel, www.cathedralpeak.co.za, tel 036 488 1888

Monk's Cowl
Champagne Castle Hotel, www.champagnecastle.co.za, tel 036 468 1063
Drakensberg Sun Hotel, www.southernsun.com,
tel 011 461 974 (Johannesburg office)

Giant's Castle
Antbear Guest House, www.antbear.co.za, tel 036 352 3143

Highmoor
Cleopatra Mountain Farmhouse, www.cleopatramountain.com,
tel 033 267 7243

Cobham
Sani Lodge Backpackers, www.sanilodge.co.za, tel 033 702 0330
Sani Pass Hotel, www.sanipasshotel.co.za, tel 033 702 1320
Cedar Garden, www.cedargarden.co.za, tel 033 701 1153
Arbuckle House B&B, arbucklehouse.co.za, tel 033 702 1990

Garden Castle
Lake Naverone, www.lakenaverone.co.za, tel 033 701 1236
Drakensberg Gardens Resort, www.goodersonleisure.co.za, tel 031 337 4222

Bushman's Nek
Bushman's Nek Berg and Trout Resort, www.bushmansnek.co.za,
tel 033 701 1236

Walking guides
In most areas of the Park, community guides can be engaged via the local KZN
Wildlife Office, or are provided by hotels. In the Cobham/Garden Castle/Bushman's
Nek area there are a number of local guides. A special recommendation can be
given for Stuart McLean, info@birdsandbeyond.co.za, tel 082 742 6981, and Paul
Roth (for overnight or longer expeditions as well as day walks),
www.highhorizons.co.za, tel 033 702 1603

For longer Drakensberg expeditions arranged from the UK consider
www.traverseline.co.uk.

APPENDIX D
Further reading

Sasol Birds of Southern Africa Sinclair, Hockey and Tarboton (Struik, 1997)

Field Guide to Mammals of Southern Africa Chris and Tilde Stuart (Struik, 2007)

Mountain Flowers: A Field Guide to the Flora of the Drakensberg and Lesotho Elsa Pooley (Flora Publications Trust, 2003)

A Complete Guide to the Snakes of Southern Africa Johan Marais (Struik, 2004)

Barrier of Spears RO Pearse (Art Publishers, 2006)

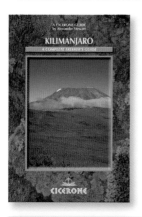
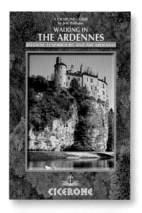
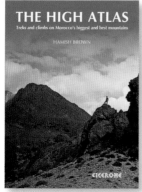

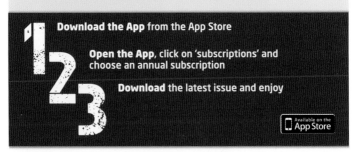

LISTING OF CICERONE GUIDES

For full information on all our
guides, books and eBooks,
visit our website:
www.cicerone.co.uk

Walking – Trekking – Mountaineering – Climbing – Cycling

Over 40 years, Cicerone have built up an outstanding collection of over 300 guides, inspiring all sorts of amazing adventures.

Every guide comes from extensive exploration and research by our expert authors, all with a passion for their subjects. They are frequently praised, endorsed and used by clubs, instructors and outdoor organisations.

All our titles can now be bought as **e-books**, **ePubs** and **Kindle** files and we also have an online magazine – **Cicerone Extra** – with features to help cyclists, climbers, walkers and trekkers choose their next adventure, at home or abroad.

Our website shows any **new information** we've had in since a book was published. Please do let us know if you find anything has changed, so that we can publish the latest details. On our **website** you'll also find great ideas and lots of detailed information about what's inside every guide and you can buy **individual routes** from many of them online.

It's easy to keep in touch with what's going on at Cicerone by getting our monthly **free e-newsletter**, which is full of offers, competitions, up-to-date information and topical articles. You can subscribe on our home page and also follow us on **Facebook** and **Twitter** or dip into our **blog**.

Cicerone – the very best guides for exploring the world.

CICERONE

2 Police Square Milnthorpe Cumbria LA7 7PY
Tel: 015395 62069 info@cicerone.co.uk
www.cicerone.co.uk and **www.cicerone-extra.com**